1

"Gigi, tell me a story"

"Gigi, Tell me a story"

Jeanette Morris

ISBN 978-84728-296-5

Table of Contents

"I could not, at any age, be content to take my place by the fireside and simply look on. Life was meant to be lived. Curiosity must be kept alive."
    -Eleanor Roosevelt

Chapter 1
Childhood 1922

The year was 1922. The date was September 6th. The time was 9am. The school bell was ringing, I have been told, when I entered this world. It was the era of the Roaring Twenties!

Two years before, the 18th Amendment had been ratified which dried up the legal use of alcohol for drinking. No liquors, wines, beer or other spirits could be manufactured, sold, given away or transported legally. Stills sprang up in secret places, speakeasies replaced saloons and fleets of trucks or cars transported the intoxicating liquors. Money was flowing as were the drinks. People were drinking more alcohol than ever before.

Not so in the house and family to which I was born. My parents were strict, devoted Baptists. Church attendance was the social life my parents enjoyed; they went every Sunday morning and evening, as well as Wednesday night Prayer service. They both sang in the choir. Dad was Superintendent of the Sunday school and a church officer. Mom played the piano for the Sunday school. Dad was a tither. First allotment from his pay envelope went into the collection envelope for church.

My first memories are of me perched on the back tank of the toilet being dressed by gentle, loving hands of the person sitting backwards on the lid of the seat. I was to learn that was not my mother. It was my sister Edith, the eldest child of our family. She was in charge of me as a toddler because a new baby had arrived. That would have been Ralph.

Leroy and Edith Hagenbucher

New babies arrived quite regularly to my parents. LeRoy
Bernhardt Hagenbucher married Edith Gertrude Plummer on
New Years Day in 1912. Edith, the first born, arrived in
December 1913. In May of 1927 Betty, the last to join our
household, came. She was brought in Dr. Marsh's black
doctor's bag. I know because I saw it. I was asleep when I
heard footsteps in the upstairs hallway. I sneaked out of my
bed and opened the door ever so slightly. Peeking out I saw
Dr. Marsh with his bag go into my parents' room. The next
morning, there she was; a brand new baby.

Betty was born just a few months after our last baby died.
Donald had not been a well baby. He had contracted
pneumonia. Most of the Helping Hand Society, the do-

12

gooders of our neighborhood, were in our kitchen that day making mustard plasters for the baby's chest and back to draw out the congestion. I was just 4 years old and underfoot. It was suggested that Mrs. Lake take me home with her. When I was brought back home it was to view Donald in his little white casket. It was the practice then to keep the deceased at home until the funeral. A big, beautiful bouquet of white roses with lots of white ribbon was hanging on our front door. I did not attend the funeral, but the following week after church and Sunday dinner, the whole family walked to Woodlawn Cemetery to visit him. We took that long walk once a week until cold weather set in.

It was our custom to use family names as middle names for the offspring. Mother sort of overdid it. We are Edith Plummer, LeRoy Plummer, Paul Plummer, Earl Plummer, Carol Plummer, Jeanette Plummer, Ralph Plummer and Elizabeth May, all with the surname of Hagenbucher.

Plummer Hagenbuchers (clockwise) Leroy, Edith, Paul, Carol, Ralph, Betty, Jeanette and Earl. Mother Edith in the middle

13

I was the sixth child in a very smooth running family. We were well organized accomplishing the necessary chores of daily living. Birthdays were celebrated with cake and ice cream with the family singing our own special birthday song. Along with one simple gift came a new job. When I became four years old I was granted the privilege of joining in the work force by helping with the drying of the breakfast dishes. "You are such a big girl now, you may help with the morning dishes." Everything was done by teams. Two people made the beds, one on each side. Another dusted the dressers and chairs. While still another ran the dust mop after the beds were completed. The last job was to dust down the stairs. All of these tasks were finished each day before we could go to school. The school bell could be heard as we hurried to get our chores done.

Mother had many tasks that she took care of while we were in school for a few hours. At noon we all returned home from school for a hot lunch that she had prepared. We then cleaned up the lunch dishes and returned to school for the afternoon session. Back home at 3:30 we started the cleanup of the downstairs, living room, and dining room. After the table was set for dinner, we could go out to play until Dad came home from work. You could set your watch by his return. Everything was very punctual. As he came up the front steps, the potatoes were being mashed in the kitchen with nary a lump! Dad would remove his coat and tie, wash up and take his seat at the head of the table. Dinner was then served, prayed over, eaten, and cleared away. One of us would be assigned to clear the table, another scraped the plates, another washed the dishes, another wiped the dishes, another put the dishes away and the last person swept the kitchen floor. You would never know ten people inhabited that house. It was that clean! I marvel at the patience of my parents to teach each one of us how to do a job and do it well. But it wasn't always pleasant. Once Mother discovered that I had missed some dust on the piano. I didn't lift the front panel and dust under it. So she stood right there and had me dust the whole room again while she watched. I didn't miss much dust after that. I soon learned it was best to do your best the first time.

My sister Carol, older than me by eighteen months, was my constant companion, playmate and friend. We jumped rope, played hopscotch, played house and played school. I always wanted to be the teacher.

Christmas was very special in a big family. On Christmas morning Mother and Dad went downstairs first. Dad would shake down the ashes in the furnace and stoke more coal on the fire. Mother would be busy in the kitchen. Not one child could start down the stairs until everyone was dressed and in line from youngest to oldest. When all were ready, Mother played a Christmas carol on the piano and we then descended the stairs. Oh! That first look at the glistening decorated tree. Next we would make a quick run to the stockings which were bulging with oranges and nuts. Then we sought out our presents. Each one of us received one toy and one new article of clothing. What fun it was.

One Christmas, Carol and I got identical Betsy Wetsy Dolls. We fed them a doll bottle of water and soon we had to change their diapers. How we loved those dolls! Later one evening, when dark had settled in, I needed to go to the bathroom. I was afraid of the dark so Carol accompanied me upstairs after turning the hall lights on. Then before I was ready she ran downstairs and turned out all the lights! I screamed and ran down after her while still carrying my Betsy Wetsy doll. I missed a step and tumbled down the stairway crashing my doll's head. Oh, how I cried! It was all her fault! Mother did not make her give me her doll even though she caused mine to be broken. Not fair!

Our house was at the crest of the hill. That made it the gathering place for down-hill sledding for all the kids in the neighborhood. Few cars were on the road and most of them avoided the steep hill. We had clear sliding for a long trip. Our street crossed a busier road at the bottom of the hill, so we used a lookout to let us know when the coast was clear. We would sail down the hill, cross the road and continue across the flats until the sled slowed to a stop. My big brother, nick-named Bud, had a set of bobsleds. They were built as sections of sleds, each with their separate set of runners. The driver could sit up front and steer the sleds. That bobsled was the joy of the crowd. Many of us could go down on it together and it traveled so fast!

As I neared my fifth birthday I was prepared for school. A clinic was held to provide vaccinations for children entering school. All had to be vaccinated against smallpox. Since Mother was left with a disfiguring scar on her upper arm where vaccinations were given, we girls were vaccinated on our upper legs where any scarring would not be visible. Short sleeves were stylish, but not short skirts. Thus the scar was hidden.

Childhood diseases were very common. One was expected to contract measles, mumps and chicken pox while young to be protected from getting the disease later in life when the illness could become more serious. Whooping cough, pneumonia, and scarlet fever were often suffered before adulthood. When there was a serious illness in a house the Health Department tacked a notice of quarantine on the front door. No one was to enter or leave. Neighbors and friends would drop off needed supplies near the door to be picked up by the family. No physical contact was made. Often the breadwinner of the household would have to stay elsewhere in order to continue working.

Perhaps those childhood illnesses which caused many absences from school were one of the reasons the school year was divided in half. Children began school in the fall and again in the spring term. In that arrangement a child who had missed too many school days in a term would

16

repeat that half year, catching up on the studies before going to the next level.

I loved school! Kindergarten, as I recall, was good. We strung a lot of big colored beads, sang songs, listened to stories and had graham crackers and milk for a snack. When I entered the first grade with Mrs. Reed as the teacher, learning began to click. The 1-1 class sat on the left side of the room while the 1-2 section was seated on the right. Each group's learning aids were in place before the proper rows of seats. It was such fun to finish my assignments quickly so I could listen, learn and do the 1-2 lessons, too. Jean Worden was in the class. She was listening to the 1-2 class the same as I was. What could Mrs. Reed do but promote both of us to the second grade room? Jean and I continued to do the same additional learning in that class. We were double promoted again! Although we devoured the second grade lessons, I was not allowed to skip another half year. Mother did not think it was right for me to be in the same class as my older sister Carol. However, Jean went on to the next class.

Sheridan Road School was a clapboard building with a bell tower. It housed six classrooms, one for each grade, and the principal's office. Each class had about 30 pupils divided into the two sections. Each desk had a seat on the front of it. When you sat at your desk you were seated on the front of the desk behind you. There was a round opening for the inkwell which was just a hole until the third grade when we learned to use scratchy, straight pens. The points were replaceable on the pen handles. It was so difficult to make ovals and do push-pulls with those miserable pens in writing class.

I remember Miss Cuallo was the music teacher. She was so beautiful! Her desk was at the end of the hallway in front of a big window. Since there was no music room, she traveled from classroom to classroom to teach. She carried the music books and a round pitch pipe. We would have to match the note she blew on her pitch pipe before starting a song. She was my absolute favorite teacher. She wore beautiful dresses with high heeled shoes. Her finger nails were long and painted. I felt those long nails when she would pinch my fat cheeks affectionately and ask if I had an apple in them. It hurt, but I loved any attention that sweet lady gave to me.

Life was most enjoyable. As long as one obeyed her parents and teachers there was nothing to fret over. I was loved, safe and secure. Little did I realize the activity that was taking place in the real world. Inventions were made and improved upon. Transportation, communication and mass production brought change quickly. Prosperity was at an all time high. Many people were investing in these new projects and making a lot of money. Entertainment flourished. With no worries and plenty of money, everyone was out for a good time. Movies began to talk, music began to syncopate, authors were prolific and travel was enjoyed.

We were the first in the neighborhood to have a radio! My dad had built one with the help of his assistant, Mom. I had no idea how it was possible to hear music out of the thin air. I only remember Mom helping Dad wrap yards and yards of wire around cylinders. I also recall some talk about the radio being a crystal set. In any event it worked! At first we put on earphones to listen. Then Dad rigged a speaker that looked like a horn-of-plenty. We could all hear the squawking and static coming from a station in Schenectady, New York, over 100 miles away, called WGY. We enjoyed music, poetry reading, The Farm and Home Hour, and a soap opera titled Myrt and Marge.

Our family had other entertainment, too. There was the Victrola. To operate it had to be wound up, a record placed on the turntable, and the needle in its armature placed in the first groove. I liked to listen to the Three Black Crows. They were so silly. One said, "Meet me on the corner tonight" The other replied, "Okay. If you get there first draw a line and if I

18

get there first I'll rub it out."

We also enjoyed a stereopticon lantern that showed pictures in three dimensions. It was a tin box with a strong light and a lens. Two identical pictures were inserted and shown as one on the screen. The screen was a white sheet hung in the archway between the dining room and the living room. The projector was placed on the dining room table. All the dining room chairs were placed in rows in the living room. Dad always ran the projector because it got so hot. We viewed the show from our seats in the living room. We saw people and places from all over. The world seemed to come alive for us.

When Mother was confined with a new baby, Dad took Edith, Bud and Paul with him on the street car to Immanuel Baptist Church which was close to the center of Syracuse. That was the church where Dad had met Mother. The younger children; Earl, Carol and I were sent around the corner on the next street for Sunday school at the Wesleyan Methodist Church. We could walk there by ourselves. Sunday school met in the sanctuary for opening exercises. Then we separated into age appropriate classes for the Bible lesson. The session ended back in the sanctuary for a closing prayer and hymn. The minister would always call for sinners to come kneel at the railing and accept Jesus as their Savior. The organist would pump out "Just As I Am" over and over until someone came forward. I can't recall how many times I got saved. I knew no one would be able to leave and go home for dinner unless someone came forward. I would get hungry, so I would get Carol to go to the railing with me in order to bring the service to an end.

We had grapevines growing along the property line. They bore heavy bunches of nice juicy concord grapes that we pressed into grape juice and bottled. Dad always provided the grape juice for church Communion Service which was observed the first Sunday of each month. Being Baptist, wine was not allowed. We children would also take grapes to school for snack time. One day in the fourth grade I was sneaking grapes into my mouth one at a time before snack time. The teacher caught me and sent me out into the hall. A short time later she came out and gave me a scolding for eating during class. Meanwhile, Carol had seen me standing in the hall. She crossed one index finger over the other index finger making the shame, shame sign to me. When the teacher said I could return to class, I wouldn't go. I told her that Carol would tell my Mother I had been naughty in school and my Mother would give me a spanking. The teacher went into Carol's classroom and spoke to her making her promise not to tell on me. Only then did I return to class.

Our small suburb of Eastwood was annexed to the city of Syracuse in 1928. The town had grown so much that needed services, available through the city, led to the small village becoming assimilated and urbanized. New schools began to be built, storm sewers were dug, police protection became available and our volunteer firemen joined the city firemen.

A Baptist Church was established on James Street across from the Catholic Church. Our parents considered joining the new congregation at the request of Edith whose friends were attending that church. However, their Immanuel Baptist Church was such an important part of their lives they preferred to remain with their old friends, but they did give Edith permission to go to the new church and take Carol and me with her. We walked the mile distance every Sunday from then on.

After that we seldom attended the old church. However, our presence was required on special days like Mother's Day. Mother always won the potted plant for having the most children in attendance. We also were needed to swell the crowd when an Evangelist preached at their church. Those were some boring evenings. I would count the light bulbs in the round circle in the dome of the ceiling over and over again.

A new school was built on Sunnycrest Road near the golf course. It was red brick with the name Aria S. Huntington School in big letters across the front at the top of the building. I never did learn who Aria S Huntington was or what he did to deserve to have his name on my new school. The new school had a room just for music, a big gymnasium and an auditorium. It was a shiny building with lots of space, but it was a longer walk from our house. That year I entered the fifth grade.

Many other changes began happening that affected the entire world. The stock exchange had collapsed. The Great Depression had arrived as the banks failed. One out of every four men was out of work. Prohibition had been repealed. I was unaware of any of this. It was more of an aura of conditions for me. Dad used to jingle his change in his pocket, passing out a nickel to each of us to run to the corner store for an ice cream on a hot night. That stopped. No new shoes were purchased when the next school year started. No new Easter finery. The paint on the house began to crack and peel. Steps and porches needed repair and replacement. Not just our house, every house! Hobos, strangers who had been hopping into boxcars to relocate looking for work, would stop at our back door for food. Mother always gave them a little something to eat as they stood outside. Mortgages on houses were being foreclosed for lack of payment. Our next door neighbor lost their house and had to move in with grandparents. At least we were assured we would have a roof over our heads because our house was free and clear of a mortgage.

It was a sad time. Everyone was poor and getting poorer, that was just the status quo. During this time school, church and the library were my hangouts. I loved to read. I could be transported to other places and other times. Mother would scold me for neglecting my household duties as I read, read,

read. My favorite author was Louisa May Alcott.

In fifth grade I was cast in the Christmas play at school. My role was the cross girl that didn't believe in Santa. I quickly learned my speaking and singing parts. We practiced every night after school on the stage in the auditorium. Unfortunately, a week before the performance calamity struck. That day when we came home for lunch, no one was home. A note from mother told us to eat the soup that was keeping warm over the coal-burning side of the stove. The note also assigned Jeanette to clean up after lunch and do the dishes. Well, there was no one there to make me do the dishes so I ran out and joined my friends walking to school. I no sooner left the house when the trolley car stopped at the bottom of the hill. Fearful that my mother had come back, we darted into a vacant tree-filled lot just up the street. I tripped on a root of a tree and fell onto a broken bottle that was standing jagged-edged upright. It cut through my snow pants, my brown ribbed long stockings, and my long winter underwear and into my lower leg. Blood gushed out. My friends helped me get back to the house. Mother had returned. She brought me in, put me in a chair and propped up my leg. While comforting me she said, "God always punishes little girls that don't obey their Mothers." Then she called the doctor to sew my leg.

My leg was tended to and bandaged but how was I to get to school? We did not have a car. Who needed one when the trolley was just a half a block away? It was too late to recast the play. Fortunately, the school janitor had a car. When the school day was finished, he came for me and carried me to school and up on the stage. Because my leg was braced in a straight position it had to be laid on a pillow. So I became a crippled, cross girl that didn't believe in Santa until the end of the play. The show must go on!

Mr. Golightly was the pastor of our Eastwood Baptist church. He was a handsome man with shiny silver hair. I believed he was sent from God. His vocabulary included words that I had never heard. I began to write down those words. When I got home I would look in the dictionary for their meanings. All afternoon (we were not allowed to leave the house or make noise on Sunday, the Sabbath) I would practice a new word or two. Once my mother chided me by saying, "You think you're pretty smart using those big words."

Mrs. Golightly led the Junior Choir. Carol and I sang in the choir. We practiced one afternoon each week after school. Several of our friends also sang in the choir. We would all walk together from school to the church. Miss Fyler was the fifth grade teacher. She was the least liked teacher I ever had. She was skinny with straight hair who wore oxford shoes. To punish a miscreant she would make her stay after school and diagram a page of sentences. Once, she had me stay on choir practice day. When I completed the sentences on my sheet, I had to take that long walk alone! I had pleaded with her to let me do my penance on another day, but no, it had to be her way.

Along about this same time Carol and I joined the church. We attended classes after school to learn about the church organization and what it meant to be a Christian. On Easter Sunday the drape was opened that revealed the tank behind the altar. Mr. Golightly was waiting for us in the water as we descended from the side. We were dressed all in white as was the minister. He asked, "Do you believe in the Lord Jesus Christ? Do you renounce all your sins?" When we replied in the affirmative, he took both of us together on one arm as we covered our noses and mouths with a folded white handkerchief and dunked us! Now we are pure in heart and spirit. After we all changed back into our Easter attire we were presented with our own Bible!

Plummer Hagenbuchers (clockwise), Leroy, Paul, Edith, Earl, Ralph, Jeanette, Carol, Betty, Edith (mother)

The decade of the 1930's was years of many failures; the stock market, the banks and the farms. The financial market already had fallen when the country was then hit by the worst drought ever. The mid-western farms dried up and literally blew away in storms of dust. Everyone was in need of help. The election of New York Governor Franklin Delano Roosevelt to the office of President of the United States with his theme song "Happy Days are Here Again" gave new hope to find solutions to the nation's problems. He declared a bank holiday to stop the money drain. Gradually he enacted other measures to put people back to work such as the Civilian Conservation Corps which built the National Park System we enjoy today.

24

Our big sister, Edith, graduated from high school at the young age of 14. She, too, loved learning and quickly completed the studies to pass state regents tests and graduated. Although her dream was to attend Syracuse University, times were too frugal. Grandma had taken a big loss on the stock market. Dad was grateful that the house mortgage was paid and he could not risk taking out further debt. She settled for Central City Business School. She attended just in the morning extending the time requirement to finish to two years when she would turn 16 and be able to accept a job.

Now with two women at home and money so tight, it was decided that Mother should go out to work in the afternoon. Mr. And Mrs. Wilkie were members of my parents' church. Mr. Wilkie worked for the city and was a prominent member of the powerful Republican Party. He used his connections and found a job for Mother, a part time janitress at one of the city schools. In gratitude of the party's generosity, she was expected to help the party when election time came around. She was asked to paste Mayor Marvin's name on hundreds of tiny colored elephant charms. We children spent hours gluing them in place.

One Sunday at church, Edith pointed out a handsome young man to Carol and me. She made fun of his name calling him Mr. Coconut. His name was Mr. Coughenour. They had met during a young people's meeting at the church earlier in the week. He asked if he could drive us home when the service was over. After a few such favors, he was invited to join the family for Sunday dinner. Everyone was nervous. Mother thought he was too old for Edith being six years her senior. He came from out of town. Even out of state. He had come to Syracuse from Pittsburgh looking for work. At least he had a job and was living with his brother in an apartment. They also owned a car together. Even though he was a very nice, polite man Mother wasn't too pleased about their friendship.

Edith and Arthur continued seeing each other. When the Sunday school had an outing, Arthur would drive Edith and her two young sisters to the event. One such picnic was at Suburban Park. I spent most of the afternoon watching the dance marathon in the covered pavilion. It was fascinating to watch the couples dancing and dancing for hours on end. The couple that lasted the longest would win a money prize. When a pair of dancers began dragging one another, the master of ceremonies would call their number and they would have to leave the floor. The live music of the band was entertaining, too. We also went on a few rides while we were at the amusement park. Back in the car for the drive home, I became violently ill. Whether it was caused by the rides, the hot dogs or the hot sun didn't matter, I just let go messing up the car very well. Poor Arthur! What he put up with to gain his fair lady.

The summer of 1934 was very busy. Carol and I became Mother's helpers. We had to do our regular assigned tasks and then fill in for Edith because she had accompanied Grandma to Europe for the summer. So Carol and I watched the baby, prepared fruits and vegetables in season for canning and during any free time we ripped the seams apart on used coats that were given to us. Although the outer nap on the wool coat was worn, the inside of the fabric looked like new. Mother spent many hours cutting and sewing coats for us from this reversed fabric. Carol and I spent most of these days together. In the evening we would sit in the platform swing and sing in harmony many of the old standard songs. The mosquitoes would drive us indoors after dark. Dad was so pleased with our cooperation he took us to the movies to see something called the Follies of 1934, our very first movie.

At this time, I was in Junior High School. The classes were held in a wing of the Eastwood High School. I was younger than the others in my grade having skipped a full year in

Elementary School. I was also quite small. All those big "men" in the school scared me. The first week I got lost and found myself in the corridor of the shop rooms. Everyone was a big, big man so I thought. They were very kind and helped me find my proper classroom.

Other changes were taking place within me. I began to have small swellings on my chest. One morning I awoke to notice stained pajama bottoms. Alarmed, I went to Mother. She told me to go to Edith. Edith took me into the darkened closet where a sanitary belt and a box of Kotex were ready. She showed me how to wear them. Not another word was said about the matter. I had no idea whether Carol had started her period or not. Those things were not mentioned in our family. My mind clicked back to an afternoon when we girls were walking to church for choir practice. Ginnie in a whispered voice asked if our mothers had told us what was soon to happen to our bodies. When we replied, "No", she added that she couldn't tell us because her mother had told her not to tell anyone whose mother hadn't told them. "Aha!" I say to myself in the closet, "This is what Ginnie was talking about."

Home had always been an organized, helpful, happy place where we each knew our responsibilities and our pleasures. But a crack began to appear. Oldest brother, Bud, did not want to obey the strict rules of conduct that were expected. He wanted to go out on school nights, drink beer and as my parents put it, carouse! This was unacceptable. There were numerous arguments and punishments put upon him which he dared to ignore. Dad put him out of the house! Mother arranged for him to sleep at a neighbors and she would feed him while Dad was at work. He continued to skip school and isolate himself. He finally left town, much to my Mother's sorrow.

Life went on. That next year (1935) Edith and Arthur were married. Edith sewed her own white lace dress, fully lined, and purchased a "picture" hat to match for her wedding. She looked like an angel; fair, slender and petite. She and Mother had also sewn dresses for Betty, Carol and me. My dress was a red plaid taffeta with a big bow tied in back. We were guests but not part of the wedding party. The reception was held in our back yard. Dad and my brothers had groomed it to perfection. We girls had helped tie little white packages of bride's cake with narrow white satin ribbon. Each guest received a package. They were to put it under their pillow at night to bring pleasant dreams.

Bud, we learned, traveled to Rochester where he secured a job at Eastman Kodak Company. He completed his High School subjects and received his diploma. He made a special trip home just to show off his Diploma. He later married Dorothy. We all went to the wedding using two cars. By this time our family owned a car that Dad drove and Arthur drove his car in order for all ten of us to attend. The Church wedding was beautiful. The bride wore a white satin gown with a long flowing train. The reception was held at the bride's home. During the party, Mother noticed many guests coming and going to the cellar. It didn't take her long to realize that booze was being served there. Immediately, she gathered her brood around her like young chickens, packed us all back in the cars and we all went home.

Chapter 2
Teen Years 1932

With the radio becoming a household fixture, we were bombarded with music. Paul Whiteman broadcast directly from the bandstand in a Chicago hotel. Although people were poor we were rich in the offerings on the radio. The other Big Bands; Benny Goodman, Tommy Dorsey, Duke Ellington, Glenn Miller and Harry James were broadcast live right into our living rooms. Comedians Jack Benny, Red Skelton, George Burns and Gracie Allen, Amos and Andy, Fibber Magee and Molly and Edgar Bergen with Charlie McCarthy entertained us weekly. Operas were offered, too, as well as "soap" operas like Helen Trent.

Dancing became my passion. Carol and I would dance together at home. Other girls would share their knowledge of the latest craze with us. Now that I was a true high school student in ninth grade, I could join in and dance in the boy's gym during the last half of lunch hour. Our family always went home for lunch, but many students ate in the cafeteria either bringing their lunches or purchasing them. Offering dancing to records in the gym made a place for the students to go while the cafeteria was cleaned up for the next shift. Our school student body needed three lunch periods to accommodate all of the students. I would run all the way home, eat as quickly as allowed and run all the way back to school to dance.

Typically the girls sat on the benches that were against the left side of the gym; while the boys stayed on the opposite side. Some boys and girls danced together. They were usually the juniors and seniors. Many girls danced together, but never did the boys pair off. One noontime, when I was in tenth grade, I entered the gym and right there was Jimmy Menapace waiting for me. He asked me to dance! That was the last time I ever danced with a girl. I loved dancing more than ever.

Jimmy became my first boyfriend. He played on the hockey team. Our family enjoyed watching the games that were played at the Coliseum on the State Fair grounds. One Friday Jimmy asked me to ride back from the game with him on the players' bus. Mother gave me permission to do so, but I must be home by twelve o'clock. What a thrill to be allowed to ride with Jimmy on the players' bus. When we arrived in Eastwood the bus stopped at the White Tower hamburger stand and let us all off. Everyone piled into this little eatery. It took a long time for everyone to be served a hamburger and a hot chocolate. It was a five block walk home after eating. Needless to say, it was past the enchanting hour when I arrived home. That ended my going on the players' bus. I had missed the curfew.

Our high school had several social groups; two sororities, one fraternity and two service clubs sponsored by the YMCA and the YWCA. Carol and I were invited to join the Beta Chi sorority. That was a bad move. Although we did do some charity work, it was mostly a social club. That was where Carol and I were introduced to cigarettes. The older girls would share with us "new" girls. Smoking is the most regrettable thing I ever did. It was not allowed at home, so I began a lot of sneaking around and hiding the things. Smoking caused a rift in my relationship with Mother. I had always been open with her and now I avoided close encounters. Once when she thought she detected the odor of smoke on us, she cried. I felt sorry, but I didn't stop!

It was the fall of 1938 that a new boy appeared in Latin III class. This was most unusual. Since the study of Latin was not that popular, the class grew smaller each semester. We learned he had returned to school after a long stay in the hospital with a strep infection of the blood. Antibiotics had not been discovered as yet, so illnesses lasted many long months if you were fortunate enough to survive.

30

He was a nicely dressed boy with dark hair, glasses covered his deep blue eyes and he had a winning smile revealing beautiful teeth. He took a liking to me! His name was Bob. Two months passed. One day as he walked past my desk and he dropped a folded flyer for me to read. It announced a formal dance that was to be held soon. On it he had written, "Will you go with me?" I replied, "I'll have to ask my mother."

Mother gave her consent. Then he said, "Will you teach me to dance?" That began our dating. Bob was a willing pupil and he soon mastered enough steps to try them on a dance floor.

Mother took me shopping for THE dress. We choose a red moiré silk with big puffy sleeves. Oh, did I feel elegant! That is until we arrived at the ballroom of the Hotel Syracuse. The Big girls were wearing strapless, slinky gowns. I just had a pretty dress. I felt just like the little kid that I was. However, the live band was playing. We danced the night away. That was the beginning of my first love. The next two years until graduation we were inseparable.

We dated just about every Friday night. We usually went to the movies, then stopped at Whittigs for a milk shake and walked home. Saturdays were often spent dancing, often at the Drumlins Country Club. I was invited to spend a week at his family's camp at Sandy Pond two or three times each summer. Swimming, speed boat riding, long walks and dancing at the local hot spots filled our time. He, being an only child, enjoyed having a steady companion and I, from a large family enjoyed being special to him.

All of the social clubs at school joined together each year to arrange for the Christmas Dance. It was the event of the year held on Christmas night in the Grand Ballroom of the Hotel Syracuse where the chairs and drapes were gold-colored and the walls were shining mirrors. Huge chandeliers hung down with fancy lights. Decorated for

Christmas it looked like fairyland.

A week before the dance a friend, Betty, asked me to go downtown with her after school because she needed to try on a dress her mother had chosen for her for the dance. On a mannequin in the store was a dress of rose-red chiffon with a full skirt and a tight-fitting bodice decorated with silver threads. It was so beautiful! I walked all around it admiring that dreamy dress. A saleslady asked me if I wanted to try it on. I said, "No, it will probably fit me and I cannot buy it." At her urging I relented and tried on the dress. Sure enough, it fit. I knew I couldn't have it. There was no money for frills. I told Mother about that most wonderful dress. On Christmas morning I opened my present and there was the dress! Unbelievable! Mother and I spent half of that Christmas Day hemming the two layers of the chiffon skirt, as well as, the taffeta underskirt. I felt like Cinderella when I went to that Christmas Ball!

School and studies and my boyfriend filled those high school years. We were required by our parents to study as a family. After the dinner table was cleared and the clean-up finished, all of us that were in high school at that time gathered around the table to do homework. There were four of us; Paul, Earl, Carol and me. Paul was left handed and seemed to make the table wiggle as he worked. That meant the rest of us often had messy, jiggly writing.

Carol and I were scheduled to a study hall the first period in the morning. Having been seated alphabetically we sat next to each other. Since both of us had completed our homework at home, there was nothing to do except chat. We had been apart at least half an hour while in separate homerooms. A lot of news about our friends could occur in that time. We were sent to the office for talking during study hall. Professor Todd could not understand how two girls that lived together, slept together in the same bed, and walked to school together could still find so much to talk about so early in the day. He just didn't know girls! The problem was solved by removing me from the study hall. I was given the task of operating the switchboard in the office for that period. Punishment? I loved it. I knew first hand all the school gossip.

Brother Paul had always enjoyed working with the Young People's Group at church. In 1938, he decided he wanted to become a minister, He liked to say that if he was going to attend church the rest of his life, it would suit him better to stand up and shout rather than sit down and shut up. He enrolled in a Baptist college in Missouri. As a result of my brother going into public life, Dad was bothered that often our surname was misspelled and mispronounced. He had it legally changed to Hagen. All the family had to be present in the lawyer's office and sign the petition. So for twenty five dollars, we changed our nationality from German American to Irish American. When school began that fall I found it a bit difficult to answer and write a changed name. I wondered if a new bride had the same trouble.

About this time a new person was added to the school staff. Mr. Kelly was hired to be the guidance counselor. It was my senior year. He introduced an achievement test for every student to take. We already had State Regents Exams to pass in order to graduate. But now in addition to the regents we had to take more exams. We sat three hours a day for three days to complete these tests. When they were scored, Mr. Kelly met with each student. He told me my scores were so high I should think about going to college. I had always wanted to be a teacher, but I knew the family funds were inadequate to send me to college. I told him so. Well, he took charge. He signed me up to take the State Scholarship test to be held soon at a downtown Syracuse high school.

I got on a bus and went downtown and took that test on the Saturday that it was given. The tests were then hand-scored while the students went to lunch. A list was posted for those

33

who did well to be interviewed by a consultant. There was my name on the list for Cortland State Teachers College. During the interview that followed, I stated that I had absolutely no money. There were no tuition charges at state colleges; however I would need to pay for my room and board. "That's alright." I was told, "We'll find you a job."

There was still plenty to attend to in my senior year of high school. Along with the usual studies was the end of the year fun. The Senior Ball was terrific. My boyfriend Bob had been elected President of the class. So, as his date, I got to lead the Grand March with him. That night I was dressed like a Southern Belle. *Gone with the Wind* had been read by everyone and the movie was all the rage. My dress was white with a boned-bodice, no shoulder straps, and a billowing hooped skirt decorated by two big red bows placed where the hoop flared the dress. I was beautiful! That was a night to remember.

Graduation Day came. We laughed, we cried. Beyond the horizon there would soon be big changes coming to our lives.

During the summer of 1939 I found employment at Woolworth's 5 & 10 cent store. I was issued a social security card. I saved enough money to pay the student fee and buy textbooks of my first year at college. As promised, an offer of a job in Cortland came. I was to be a mother's helper in a small family.

Meanwhile Bob had been accepted at Syracuse University. We would no longer be in the same school or the same town. After much thought, we both realized it was not practical to still go steady. Neither one of us wanted to sit back and not participate in college life. I returned his fraternity pin while shedding a tear. We still dated all summer. We spent a week with his parents at their camp. We still cared for each other.

Chapter 3

Cortland 1938

September came. It was the beginning of a new life and I was not even seventeen. I was driven to Cortland State Teacher's College by my parents. We arrived at my new home, a two-bedroom bungalow owned by a family of four. I was very unhappy when they drove away. Right away I knew I would not be happy in this house. I got a make-shift room in the attic. One daughter was my same age and in high school. The other daughter was ten. I was to serve them in the dining room while I ate in the kitchen. Never had I been treated like a maid! A maid that had to sleep in the attic! I thought those two lazy girls should be helping their mother. They didn't need me. They were just putting on airs by hiring a maid!

Cortland College 1939

I was very lonely. No big family. No friends. No boyfriend! Alone! I cried myself to sleep most nights. My only solace was my daily letter from Bob. I wrote to him each day, too. Never would I let on that I couldn't make it. The studies posed no problem. It wasn't the housework, I was raised doing that. It was the way the family treated me, not the least bit friendly. They were trying to be classy when they really had no class.

Just before Thanksgiving recess, I changed all that. Through the grapevine I heard of a family who needed help. Their student helper was going out to do her student teaching. She was a senior and would not be returning to live with them. I walked to the house, rang the bell and offered my services. It was a lovely home. There was an eight year old girl, Mary Elizabeth, and a two year old girl, Patsy. Mr. Hayes told me to pack my belongings and to tell the other family I was leaving. He came Friday night to collect me and my few belongings. What a difference! The room I was given was big with a walk-in closet. The furniture was antique curly maple sleigh-end bed, chest of drawers, dressing table with a stool and a desk. That was more like the way I wanted to live.

My duties were very simple. Yes, I still had to clean the house on Saturday and help serve the dinner, but now I sat with the family in the dining room to eat. I was seated next to Patsy to help her with her meal. When the dishes were done and the dining room in order, I was free to go out or go upstairs to study. If I were needed to stay with the children in the evening while their parents went out, I was paid by the hour in cash. Once again I felt like a respected member of a family.

Patsy, a vibrant, curly haired redhead took to me. She waited all day for me to come home from class. She would not let her mother or anyone comb her hair but me. That was my first task upon arrival home each day. Then I played with her and Mary Elizabeth until it was time to set the dinner table. We became really good friends. I stayed with that family for three years until Mr. Hayes was transferred and the family moved out of town.

Everything was better then. On Friday night once each month the college held what were called Mixers. That's just what we did, mixed with one another dancing to a terrific band lead by Spiegle Wilcox. Right away I was invited to dance. It was best to go alone to the Mixer so you could accept all the dance offers.

Bob was still my main boyfriend. He invited me to attend his fraternity dances at Syracuse University and he came to my school dances. However, the letter writing gradually slowed down. We dated every holiday when I returned home from school. During sophomore year, we both started seeing someone else and our romance faded as our common interests became different.

My new romance came about in a strange way. I was going out with Rol, a really fun guy. He lived in the rooming and boarding house run by the Morris family. In order for their son, Goodwin, a junior in college, to finance his room and board the Morris family rented a big house and let out rooms to other students. They also served meals. Rol and Monk (Goodwin's nickname) were roommates. So I saw a lot of Monk while dating Rol.

When Rol had to leave for his assignment of student teaching, Monk said he would take care of his girl. The very first weekend night, that Rol was gone Monk took me to the movies. I had been unaware that Monk had had a crush on me for some time. Now he made his move. He hardly let me out of his sight. I was flattered. When Rol came in town on a Saturday, I was out with Monk. Rol was furious because I didn't change my plans and go out with him. He dropped me

37

like a hot potato. Now Monk had no competition. Although we enjoyed being together, walking, dancing, studying or attending school events, I found him too possessive. He never ended one date without a promise of the next. I had no time for myself or girlfriends. When the school year ended I broke it off. He claimed he would marry me someday.

It was the summer of 1940. The war in Europe was an ocean away. Hitler had come to power and was expanding his borders by overthrowing Poland, Scandinavia, France and threatening England. The United States geared up for war. Congress passed the Selective Service Act. All males eighteen years of age had to sign up for the draft. Each county in the state was given a quota of inductees to fill. Cortland County had all of the college men sign up so when their new quotas came in they called up the college men instead of their own fair sons.

School was out for the summer. Monk had worked in the vegetable canning factory near his hometown and had earned a fair amount of money by working long, long hours during the pea, bean and corn season. He came to Syracuse to tell me he would soon leave for the Army Reception Center. He wanted to get married right then. There was no way I wanted to marry. Besides, my mother did not approve of my taking up with a "fella" from school whose family, church and background she knew nothing about. It was best that we go our separate ways. He was not a happy person. His life was not going the way he hoped.

George Goodwin Morris was born in Warsaw, NY in the year 1919. He came from generations of George Morrises. His father was George William. His grandfather was George Alfred. To distinguish one George from another he was called Goodwin. The family lived a comfortable life as the owners of a successful tailoring business providing handmade suits for the wealthy men in the surrounding communities including the big city, Rochester. Doctors, lawyers, government office holders and business men were their clientele. Even young Goodwin wore tailor made outfits. Goodwin was an only child for three years, he was adored by all. A sister, Mildred, was born and then a brother, Gordon. Even at an early age Goodwin was devoted to the outdoors and sports. He was a Boy Scout, eventually earning the honor of Eagle. He and his buddies enjoyed every sport as the seasons came and went. They camped out near Silver Lake most of the summer fishing, roaming the woods, and roasting potatoes from a nearby farmer's field. There he gained the nickname, Monk, as they dubbed each other with an animal nickname. He loved fishing, having been introduced to stream fishing when his father carried him on his shoulders to go to nearby Oatka Creek. His dad also took him small game hunting.

Life was swell. Too good to last. The Oatka Creek overflowed its banks flooding their house. Water reached the second floor from which they had to be rescued. Young Gordon was stricken with an infection of the blood. He was hospitalized for months. The bills added up. The final blow was the Great Depression that caused the demise of their business. They experienced hard times.

George William Morris found employment as an instructor of tailoring at the State Prison in Wallkill, NY on the Hudson River. The family moved to the eastern part of the state. They were so unhappy. The terrain was different, the people were different. The schools were different. Goodwin was a sophomore in high school when they pulled up stakes and moved.

He entered school after the semester was well underway. The history class was taking a test on his first day. The teacher said he didn't have to do the test because he was new to the class. For lack of something thing else to do, he did the test. He earned the highest mark of the class! He couldn't believe how disrespectful the students were and that they didn't do their homework assignments. He went out for the sport of track, and ran the high hurdles. He tried, but he missed the idyllic life he was used to living back home in Warsaw. He was so miserable his family let him return to Warsaw to live with his maternal grandmother and complete high school with his friends.

It was back home with his friends and his sports that he learned about attending state colleges. His coach had graduated from a state college and guided him through the requirements. He was accepted for his academic record and his sports ability. He entered Cortland State College the year before I did.

1941 was a turbulent year, personally and world-wide. The world was embroiled with Hitler's invasions. Franklin Delano Roosevelt was serving his third term as President. America was getting closer to war. We were engaged in shipping goods to England on a lend lease basis to support the war effort. German submarines were torpedoing our ships. To protect these ships, America began sending warships to guard them. American factories began retooling and gearing up to manufacture war materiel.

I returned to Cortland State for my Junior Year. There never were many male students at the college because it was a teacher preparation school. Most of the men were in the Physical Education major. Now there were so few men on campus it may as well have been an all girls' school. Our spare time was filled writing to the men in service. I dated a town boy a little. He was the cousin of a friend that sang with me in the Women's Glee Club. Mary arranged the blind date. His name was Bob. What a great dancer he was! Most of our dates were trips to the Johnson City Pavilion forty miles away where the Big Bands made one night stands en route to Chicago from New York City. We danced to the best of them. Bob and I were just dance partners. We could really "cut a rug".

Meanwhile Monk has been inducted into the Service at Buffalo and was in basic training. We exchanged a few letters. Then he was sent to the Washington state where he became a cadet in the Army Air Force. The Air Force was looking for college men to become pilots and officers. He almost didn't qualify because of a high blood pressure reading. He was put to bed to rest until the pressure returned to the normal range. Thus he was accepted. He was then sent for pilot training in Arkansas. George moved around so much, I stopped writing. It was hard to know his latest address. He wouldn't accept that. He sent me a Special Delivery letter that came to me in class. In it he chastised me for not writing, saying he waited every mail call for a letter from me. He made me feel so guilty and self-centered; I immediately wrote to him and continued all through the war.

He found it difficult to tell me he had flunked out of pilot training. He had never failed anything in his life. It was a problem with depth perception of his eyes that make it difficult to land the aircraft smoothly and safely. He was then sent to Midland, Texas for bombardier training. It was while he was there that Japan bombed Pearl Harbor on December 7, 1941. Immediately, every serviceman had to send his civilian clothes home and every leave was cancelled. War was declared! President Roosevelt called it "A date which will live in infamy."

Then our letters became serious. We realized we were unable to make plans. All leaves cancelled, we couldn't even see one another. He suggested I travel to visit him. Of course, my mother put her foot down to that idea. So he asked his mother to escort me to visit him. She was happy to have the opportunity of seeing her son. Although Mother never gave me permission to go, she didn't stop me.

It was a long, grueling bus trip from New York City to

41

Midland, Texas. Three days and two nights after we started we arrived in west Texas. There he was! He was so happy and nervous; he didn't know whom to kiss first, his mother or his girlfriend. In order to be admitted to the training base one had to be related to the cadet. That posed a problem. He couldn't get off base and I couldn't get on. He quickly solved that problem. On my clearance papers he wrote relationship: fiancée. That is how we became engaged.

When I returned home to Syracuse I broke the news to my parents that we were engaged. You would think I had admitted to murdering someone. Mother was beside herself. She posed so many questions: Why would you want to get married if you can't be together? Why would you want to get married if you can't have a home? Why would you want to get married if you couldn't have a family? She just didn't get the fact that we were in love and wanted to spend together what little time there was before he was sent to war. It was a stormy summer. At last I was allowed to accept his ring which he sent for our birthday. Yes, we shared the same birthday, September 6th.

I had appealed to my sister Carol to help me with my decision. She had her diamond from Red, her future husband. Somehow she could do things I wasn't allowed. She backed out of giving any advice, she claimed only I could choose between Mother saying, "No! No!" and Monk calling begging me to say, "Yes". It was only later that I learned that Carol and Red had been secretly married before he left for Service.

That summer I had the job of recreation director at the Northside playground in Syracuse. When fall came I returned for my senior year at Cortland State. I was required to student teach during the first semester of my senior year. I was assigned to a fourth grade class at McGraw, a small town just outside of Cortland. Meanwhile, Monk has graduated from bombardier school and was commissioned a

Second Lieutenant. He was assigned to the air base at Columbia, South Carolina. With a paycheck of $125 a month, he could now support a wife. His long-distance calls were numerous, always asking me to come visit him.

Chapter 4
War Bride 1942

A teachers' conference was held the first week in October so school was closed for an extra day. Student teachers were not required to attend so we made plans for me to go to Columbia. We were so happy to be together again. He took me to visit the men whom I had met as cadets in Midland, Texas. Several of them had married their girl back home and had set up housekeeping. When he returned me to the hotel, I said, "Let's do it. Let's get married." The next day we got the license. We could have been married by the Justice of the Peace right then, but I insisted we be married in a church. That night, at 8 o'clock October 5, we were married by the Reverend F. Clyde Helms in the Shandon Baptist Church in Columbia, South Carolina.

Wedding Photo 1942

A party was held at the Officers' Club. We had a wonderful time. Monk wanted to share the news with his parents. He sent them a telegram. I sent my parents the same. My poor parents were awakened in the middle of the night with what they considered terrible news.

We spent the night in the hotel room where I had been staying. He had to go to the air base the next morning. When he returned in late afternoon, we moved into a room he had rented for five dollars a week in a lovely private home. We walked to a little café nearby for dinner. He bought a meal plan for the rest of the month. He had taken care of everything: a place to sleep and food to eat,- that was all we needed. We spent the rest of the month there while looking for better quarters. We were able to sublease an apartment that was vacated when a serviceman was reassigned. It was in a nice, nearly new apartment complex. We took over where the last couple left off. The furniture was already rented, the dishes were in the cupboards and the utilities were working. We had to pack up their extra clothing and linens that they were unable to take with them and ship them to the address they would later send us. We felt fortunate to have good luck to find such nice living quarters so quickly. We stayed there for nine full months before he was reassigned.

That sure was a long, long honeymoon! We were so happy. I wrote to both of our parents each week. My parents never answered a single letter. I didn't have much to do to fill my time. There was little house keeping with just two people. However, I did have to learn to cook because mother had done all the cooking. The girls' job at home was cleaning up after dinner and keeping the house. George was wonderful; he ate all the flops and only complained about the coffee. I never drank coffee, I didn't know what good coffee tasted like, and even today I still don't make it very well.

The young wives spent a lot of their time playing bridge. I

knew a few card games but not bridge. I went to a bookstore and bought a bridge workbook. While the others played cards, I studied and did the work sheets at home until I learned the game. I was invited to join in and play at the club on Thursday afternoons. I also went to the Red Cross center where we rolled bandages and knit scarves. A few hours each week were spent at the Filter Center. We plotted the airplanes that appeared on the scouting screen. We would include the number of engines and wings and insignia. We plotted blips on a huge map of the area following the paths of the airplanes. This was part of the Civilian Defense program. In my spare time I knitted wool socks for my husband.

The months passed quickly. George's mother came down to visit and taught me to drive the car we had bought. George got too tense trying to teach me. I was then able to help with the long drive when Monk received orders to report to the Replacement Center in Salt Lake City. Not knowing where he would be assigned, stateside or overseas, he suggested I return home. This was a trial period to see if it would be possible to stay with my parents if or when he was shipped out. Together George and I drove to his home in Warsaw. He boarded the train in Buffalo and continued to his destination. Alone, I drove on to Syracuse to face my parents.

It was a warm, sunny pleasant Sunday. I pulled up in front of the house and entered the front door. No one was in sight. Passing through the house I saw Mom and Dad sitting in the back yard. I came up behind them and said, "Hello!" No response. I commented on the beauty of the flowers and trees and grass. No Response. Finally, I turned to return to the car. Mother got up and followed me demanding to know where I was going. "Someplace where I am welcome," was my reply. She reached in the back seat and took out a suitcase saying, "Well you're our daughter you will stay here". There was very little conversation at supper. Dad had still

46

not spoken to me. Betty, the last child at home, was the only other person at that once crowded table.

Surprise! Surprise! The next morning everyone was chatting together. I found out that the immediate cause of the cool reception was a neighbor lady. While noticing the boxes of things arriving by mail, she had commented to Mother that Jeanette must be returning to have a baby. That would have been the ultimate shame for a daughter to have had to get married. I was far from expecting. In fact I didn't weigh one hundred pounds!

Three days later a telegraph came from Monk. He had been assigned to a post at Boise, Idaho. He wanted me to come at once. Dad took me to the train and saw me off telling me to call if I needed anything. Another long ride on the train and we were together again. We stayed in a motel for a few days. We ate at the Officers' Mess. I could not eat. There were so many cockroaches scampering along the tables. The men were actually taking bets on which one would cross a line first.

Rod McClennan and his wife Evelyn from Columbia were also there. Three days later both Rod and Monk were to report to Wendover, Utah assigned to a new bomb group just being formed. They had their car and invited us to join them on the trip to the new base. It was beautiful traveling through the Rocky Mountains.

Arriving at our destination, Wendover Air Base on the salt flats of Utah near the Nevada line, the men reported for duty and were assigned bachelor's quarters in the barracks. There was nothing available for wives or sweethearts. Not far west from the base was the Stateline Motel. We tried to get a room there but it was already filled by the higher echelons' wives. There were WAC quarters on the base. They could not allow guests to stay. It looked like Evelyn and I would be spending the night sleeping in the car. The men went to their assigned sleeping quarters,

Evelyn and I went back to the Stateline Hotel for a Coke. Straddling the state lines of Utah and Nevada, gambling was allowed in the Nevada side and a restaurant was on the Utah side. We were sitting in the restaurant sipping our Cokes when a man stopped by our booth. He said he was a dealer for one of the gambling tables. He asked how it was that two pretty young girls (I was 21) were alone out there in the wilderness. We told him about our predicament. He left only to return to give us the key to his room. He had asked a fellow worker if he could bunk in with him so we girls could have a place to sleep.

The next morning after breakfasting with our husbands, it was decided that we girls should go to the only nearby city and find a place to stay. The city, Salt Lake City, was a fifty mile drive east over a lonely desert road. There was not even a filling station along the way. We found a studio apartment near the heart of the city not far from Temple Square. A sitting room with a Murphy bed, a tiny kitchenette and an even smaller bathroom became our home.

Evelyn soon found work as a stenographer for traveling business men who would stay at the Zion Hotel. I took a part time position selling records at the Zion Mercantile store. The store had listening booths where you could listen to the music. Duke Ellington's Satin Doll was played constantly. Often Evelyn would call me to have lunch with her and her current boss in the hotel dining room. There also was another Air Force wife staying at the hotel. She was very pregnant. We would check on her twice a day. We urged her to return to Texas while she still could travel. She refused saying that she wanted her husband to see their baby before he went overseas. He did.

On the first Sunday Evelyn and I drove to the Air Base to see our men. When Monk and Rod brought us back they kept the

48

car. That way when one or the other man got a day off he could drive in to see his wife. When that happened the other wife would go out for a long, long walk giving the couple some privacy time.

One evening I heard big band music drifting in our open window. I suggested to Evelyn that we go looking for it. It couldn't be too far away if we could hear it so well. Within the block we found a USO Club. We entered and were soon caught up in the entertainment. That became our hangout. We both loved to dance and there were lots of soldiers who needed partners.

As more and more men arrived at the base accompanied by their wives it became necessary to open a newly built barracks for the women to stay in. Our husbands arranged for us to move there. It was a regular barracks, just like the men slept in. A large room filled with bunked beds. I chose a top bunk. I didn't want dust and lint falling in my face from above. I had had to use public showers before, but in these there were women walking around nude. I was aghast at the size of some of them. Evelyn and I were both tiny women; short and thin without very big adornments. Some of these women looked like Amazons to us. We showered quickly, wrapped up in a towel and sought some privacy to dress.

Our days then were spent in the Officers' Club. There was no work on base. We played a lot of card games and listened to the radio and waited for our husbands to come and eat with us. They were flying day and night to prepare for conflict. When they were free for a night, a strange procession left the wives' barracks and disappeared in the desert hills. Each couple carried an itchy, scratchy army blanket upon which to retire. With no light except the moon and the stars, one stepped gingerly avoiding cacti and copulating couples.

Three months and it was time to move again. A new flight

group was forming in Fairmont, Nebraska. Monk was assigned as the Lead Bombardier of the 726th Squadron and Rod was made Lead Bombardier of the 725th Squadron. They were promoted to 1st Lieutenants. As before, we all traveled in the Mc Lennons' car. The landscape had changed again. The barren earth had become lush cornfields stretching for miles upon endless miles. After checking in at the base, we were able to locate lodging in a large farmhouse. Two furnished bedrooms with a shared bath were available. We rented them. The landlord was a man in his 40's who was a civilian employee at the base. He and his wife had six children. It was a full house.

The 451st Group was assembled to be deployed overseas. Now they really trained day and night. Evelyn and I kept each other company. A last leave was given before shipping out. Monk and I traveled by train back home to New York. After a brief stay, we drove our car back to Nebraska. It was much more convenient to have our own transportation.

One beautiful, cool, crisp, sunny October day Monk came home at noon. He had checked out a shotgun to go hunting. He had often remarked that here he was in the best pheasant hunting country and he was unable to take advantage of it. That afternoon we drove to the cornfields. We started walking between the rows of corn. The pheasants flew out but they flushed too close to his feet for him to get a shot. He suggested that maybe I could run down the rows ahead of him to flush out the pheasants. So off I went barking like a bird dog. It worked. He bagged enough pheasants for Betty, the landlord's wife, to prepare a delicious meal for us and her whole family.

We had been married more than a year and there was still no baby on the way. I desperately wanted one. In those sentimental, bittersweet days, the thought of the possibility of his not returning was real. I needed his child and he should leave progeny. George's final move was now

50

scheduled. We moved on to Lincoln, Nebraska to the Cornhusker Hotel which had been taken over by the Army. There was no training for the men here. They reported daily to the base to see if orders had been cut for them to fly out. They would return by mid-morning in time for the wives to join them for brunch. A live band played every evening. It was delightful to have so much time together again to enjoy.

Monk arranged for the sale of the car. He also decided along with several others to send the wives home before shipping out. The first of December was the date set for the wives' departure. Reality was setting in. This was it! Monk appeared and acted the same as always except at night. He sweated so heavily the bed was wet. I knew he was scared, but outwardly he showed no signs of it. On the morning of December 1, 1943 we said our goodbyes as he left to report to the base. I then gathered myself together and went down the elevator along with a few other wives. As we stepped out of the elevator we were met by an officer who said, "They've gone, girls. They flew out this morning."

Chapter 5
War Years 1943

It was a sad trip home. When I arrived, my brother Earl was on leave from the infantry. He was wearing his officers' uniform. I almost collapsed with grief. I cried for days and days. I couldn't keep any food down. On Sunday the family attended church without me. Edith was visiting with her two little children. She coaxed me out of bed and encouraged me to eat something. Immediately, I was ill. She solved my predicament by saying I think you're pregnant. That changed my outlook. At once I began to feel better and even joyous over the possibility. A visit to the doctor that week confirmed my pregnancy. I was overjoyed. It was a culmination of our love.

I wrote and wrote daily letters to the Daddy-to-be. I received daily V-mail letters from him but no mention of the good news. I was sending letters to his APO number in Italy where he was assigned. I did not know where he was or how he got there. As it turned out, the group flew from Lincoln, Nebraska to Miami, Florida, then to Brazil and over to Morocco, Africa. They were stationed in North Africa for a few months. The group received no mail. They were not allowed to say anything in their letters giving away any information that could be harmful. All communication was heavily censored.

Everyone was doing their best for the war effort. War Bonds were being hawked by movie stars. Big bands were playing dance music in big ballrooms filled with the soldiers when they returned. Communities were staging black-out practices. When the factory whistles blew in the night all lights had to be extinguished. A warden from each neighborhood would walk his beat checking. Anyone caught with any flicker of light was fined. Ration books were distributed by the government. Blue coupons were for canned goods. Red coupons were for meat, butter, and cheese. The allowed amounts varied as supplies became available. Each person in a household was allowed a coupon for two pounds of canned foods per month. The red coupon was for twenty ounces of meat and four ounces of cheese each month. Already sugar and shoes were rationed. The gas shortage put an end to pleasure driving. One had to have a sticker denoting they were a defense worker in order to buy gas. Everyone grew a vegetable garden called a Victory Garden. If you wanted to eat you had better work for your food.

One airman, while unloading a cargo plane with supplies noticed a bag of mail destined to their APO number. He stole the bag of mail. In it was a letter from me saying, "I'm booming along into motherhood." His reply to that letter commented on the fact that we had tried so long and then made the connection at the last minute. Always conscious that someone was reading what he was writing, he added, "I'll bet the censors are enjoying this." When I received the letter the censor had written in the margin, "I read far worse, congratulations."

It wasn't long before my clothes began to be tight around my swelling body. Mother accompanied me downtown to purchase maternity dresses and undergarments. Before we left the store, she directed me to the millinery department where she began popping cute little hats on my head one at a time. She chose a dark brown straw hat with white ruching around the edge of the narrow brim. As we left the store with that silly hat perched on my head she announced, "There now, people will look at your hat and not your bulging belly."

I knew absolutely nothing about having a baby. They just came in our family. Mother chose Dr. Marsh, our family doctor when I was younger, who now was a gynecologist. Mother always went with me for my regular pregnancy check-ups. She and Dr. Marsh visited while I and the nurse were in the examining room. It was as if I wasn't even present. When the doctor told me that he would call me when he wanted me to come to the hospital, I thought that was strange. I thought there was always a last minute rush to get there on time. Mother and the doctor decided I should have a delivery by cesarean section because my frame was so small. Later he called to tell Mother that I could deliver naturally.

On June 22nd I began to feel a tightening in my stomach area, but then it would subside. I told Mother and she suggested I write down the times whenever I felt the tightening. They came five minutes apart. She decided it was time to go to the hospital. When we came to the maternity ward I could hear some loud noises sounding like someone was in pain. I couldn't understand that. I had no pain. "That's good," said Mother. She stayed with me all afternoon while I was being prepped. (I never knew you had to be shaved down there!) Mother went home for supper. While she was gone something burst and I was wet! I rang for the nurse. She told me my water broke. (What was that?) So many nurses were needed for the war that they were scarce in the hospitals at home. She left and then I soon found out what the other mothers-to-be were yelling about. I joined the chorus loud and clear. With difficulty I was moved onto a gurney and taken to the Delivery Room. I good whiff of ether and I was out of it. The next morning I saw our beautiful baby boy. He was perfect. Mother sent a cable to the Daddy that all was well. He won five dollars on a bet he would have a boy.

Baby Jimmy 1944

When I was resting in the hospital, an article appeared in the newspaper. George G. Morris had received the Distinguished Flying Cross and was promoted to Captain. He had led a very successful bombing raid on the German oil supply. A picture of him was printed along with an interview. When he was asked if he were superstitious, He answered, "No, but I never fly without wearing the socks my wife knit for me."
How proud I was

Receiving the Distinguished
Flying Cross 1944

55

Lucky socks 1944

Jimmy was six weeks old when Monk came home for rest and return. We felt strange with one another. I was not back to shape and felt embarrassed. He didn't know how fragile I would be. So we spent the whole first night just looking at our baby. We soon got over our shyness. He had two weeks leave. We borrowed a car, packed up our baby and went to Eagle Bay in the Adirondack Mts.

When his leave time was up we drove to the Morris's and left baby Jimmy with them while we went to Atlantic City where he had orders to report. Again the army had taken over a hotel for quarters. It was the Claridge Hotel on the Boardwalk. This was another heart wrenching time. He had been promoted and assigned to 49th Bombardment Wing Headquarters in Italy. Could he return safely again?

I returned to Syracuse to my parents and baby. A long, hard

winter set in. In spite of being surrounded with family and friends, I was lonely. We corresponded every day. He was unable to mention anything about where he was or what he was doing. He had returned to the war to lead missions over Ploesti, Romania and Bucharest, Hungary four times, Munich three times, Weiner Neustadt two, and Vienna once. He flew fifty-two bombing missions in all without a scratch. He earned two Distinguished Flying Crosses and a Presidential Citation for the Group. Missions accomplished, George returned home February 1945.

With the rank of Major, Monk was too highly commissioned to be assigned to a unit, so he was designated Ground Safety Officer at Westover Air Base at Chicopee, Massachusetts. He located an apartment for his family and came for Jimmy and me. Life was very similar to civilian living. He would leave for work at the base in the morning and return for dinner in the evening. I really enjoyed being a family and living together.

In April 1945 our beloved President, Franklin Delano Roosevelt died suddenly of a cerebral hemorrhage. Our country mourned openly at the news. There was weeping in the streets, on trains and busses, at the military establishments, in our homes, churches and in our public buildings. It was a solemn time. Harry S Truman, vice president, was sworn in as the new president.

Just a month later Germany signed an agreement of unconditional surrender in Rheims on May 7, 1945. The news reached the jubilant world on May 8th, VE Day. We celebrated at the Officers' Club on the base singing and dancing. "Chattanooga Choo Choo" was the song of the night. "Chattanooga Choo Choo won't you choo choo me home?"

It wasn't long when I discovered that I was pregnant again. I was not delighted. We were living in furnished quarters; we owned nothing but a car, clothes, sheets and towels! This was not the time to be having more children. We were living like gypsies—everything was transient. I was upset and crying all the time. A week later he presented me with a complete set of sterling silver, service for eight, all with our monogram etched on the handles. He had purchased them at the Hall Gallery downtown. "Now do feel you have roots?" he asked.

The war with Japan was still waging. Stories of hand to hand combat to win islands in the Pacific filled the news. Iwo Jima was taken with the loss of over 68,000 lives of U.S. Marines and 23,000 Japanese defenders. The ghastly high tolls of lives prompted people to demand a quick end to the conflict. President Truman, as commander-in-chief, ordered the dropping of the atomic bomb, the newest weapon in our arsenal. The bomb had taken over two years and $2 billion to develop. Japan had been issued an ultimatum by the Allied Nations' leaders, Churchill, Stalin and Truman, to surrender or suffer annihilation. The bomb was dropped from a B29 bomber named the Enola Gay after the pilot's mother. The devastation was complete, 140,000 people from a city population of 350,000 were dead. Anything within a 2 mile radius of the bomb epicenter was incinerated.

A second bomb was released over Nagasaki three days later. Emperor Hirohito and his war council surrendered officially aboard the battleship Missouri on September 2, 1945. World War II had ended!

Chapter 6
Growing a Family 1945

The scramble was on! Every Army Air Force member began getting their papers together and counting up points towards mustering out. Knowing the fields of employment will be swamped with applicants eager to establish their futures in peace time, the men scurried to get appointments for review and orders to leave the service. Monk was among them. He still had his last year of college to complete before applying for a teaching position. We had our very first heated arguments. His pay was so good I couldn't see giving it up until he was forced to do so. He argued that his commission was a Reserve Commission; therefore he would be knocked back to a non-com status and low pay. He felt he must return to civilian life as soon as possible and get started on his peacetime career. All the good teaching positions would be filled.

He won me over to his side of the argument. In less than two weeks' time he was back in college for his senior year at Cortland and I was back living with my family forty miles away in Syracuse. Within a month he had located a furnished flat for us to be together. He had also obtained a half-time job teaching and coaching at the nearby small town of Groton. The only part time about the job was the pay. All the boys' gym classes were scheduled during the afternoon while he was at the high school and then the teams practiced until six o'clock. Groton School District got a full time teacher and coach for half price.

It was a fun time being back at college. Many of the students that had been drafted for service returned with their wives and infants to complete their courses of study. We had numerous friends that spent time with us. Once again we went to dances, played cards and had pot-luck suppers. George's mornings were spent in classes, home for lunch at noon, off for a full afternoon of teaching and back home for dinner late in the evening. It was a good life, and most of it was paid for by the GI Bill.

On March 2 of 1946 our second son, Thomas was born. That was tough on Monk. He had coached a basketball game that evening, arriving home at 10 o'clock. We enjoyed a late snack together and prepared for bed when I felt a contraction. This time I knew what was going on. He went out to warm the car on the bitter cold winter night before he helped me into the car. Jimmy had already been taken to Syracuse to   visit with my mother and father. The streets were rough with rutted ice. Fortunately we made it to the hospital in time. Monk stayed in the waiting room as all men did back then. It was right next to the nursery. He said all the babies were crying and they all sounded like they were calling, "Monk, Monk". Just past midnight our new baby boy was born. New mothers were kept in the hospital for ten days to two weeks on bed rest to recover. By the time Tommy and I were discharged, spring had arrived. The sap buckets were hanging from the maple trees, the sun was warming the earth, crocuses and daffodils were blooming. It was like I had reentered life!

Baby Tommy was a very good baby. He slept and ate and giggled and cooed. Jimmy was the handful. Just 20 months old, full of energy and curiosity, he took most of my time. There was reading books and playing together. He always wanted company. It was a task to take the boys out for a walk. To get both of them ready and outside on a chilly spring day was a chore. Jimmy would run away as soon as his feet hit the sidewalk. Shopping was impossible. I settled that problem by purchasing a harness for him. He was on a tether strap and could go just a few feet from me. However, when I would put on the harness, he would squat down and not move! After that I did all my shopping alone when their Dad was home to stay with the two young boys.

The college graduation was held in May 1946. George (no

longer called Monk) accepted a physical education teaching position in Endwell, New York, a small growing community along the Susquehanna River west of Binghamton. We went there looking for a place to live. We were quickly faced with the reality that millions of servicemen like George had returned from the war looking for a home in which to settle down and raise a family. There was nothing for sale. Most landlords would not rent to children because they might mark up the walls. We could not find a house.

A real estate saleswoman suggested we look in the countryside. She had a listing for a house 20 miles away in Triangle, New York. The present owner had worked in Binghamton and was retiring and moving to Florida. Following her directions we traveled north up route 11 to Whitney Point, turned right onto route 206 to Triangle, then turned left up North Street. One more mile and there it was.

A big beautiful white farmhouse situated on a knoll overlooking the lush May countryside. A huge catalpa tree was bursting with creamy blossoms, a crab apple tree was bright with red flowers, a curving driveway was edged with remnants of hundreds of spring bulbs. "I want this", I whispered as we climbed out of the car.

We moved in within a month. The Smiths from whom we purchased the property had gutted the eighty-year-old house and remodeled the whole main floor. The second level was floorless. The stairway led to the empty second floor, a large vacant space with bare studs. It was ready to be finished off for more bedrooms and a bath. However, the first floor that was newly completed had a full bath and a huge bedroom, large enough for our whole family. Another plus was that the furniture (except for the bedroom suite) was included in the sale. We shopped in Syracuse for a Stickley solid cherry four poster bed and dresser. The bed and dresser was delivered into the large bedroom where both cribs had already been set up. We were home! We owned a house

61

with a mortgage, a big barn, an iron-wheeled tractor, chicken coops, tools and sixty five acres of hillside.

We hosted many friends and family that summer. It was a beautiful location, the scenery idyllic, the country breeze was refreshing and they were all anxious to observe the new farmers. One friend, Ruth and her husband Bill brought along a farm magazine to give us. It was presented in jest to the city sophisticates out on the farm. Little did they realize how important the information in that periodical would soon become.

Before the Smiths had sold the place, they had agreed to take a cow for the winter while the owner took his ailing son to Arizona. The Smiths decided not to inform the cow's owner of the sale of the property. They observed that we had two babies and we could probably use the milk. One day late in summer Dolly cow was brought into the barn. The problem to solve was how to milk her. In the magazine that Ruth and Bill had given to us were pictures and directions on the proper way to milk a cow. We tacked the article onto Dolly's stall. We each found a stool in the barn and sat down, one on each side of the cow. With each of us looking at the illustration we began to try our hand at milking. I took two udders and George the other two. The directions said to squeeze from the top down. I did pretty well. George, however, kept squeezing from the bottom up and no milk came. Dolly had very small udders. It was hard to get a good hand on them. However, with practice and patience we managed to milk the cow. She was a good "milker". We had buckets, pails and pans filled with milk. Anyone who crossed our threshold had to drink milk and lots of it. I soon learned how to churn butter and how to make cottage cheese. Pretty incredible for a girl raised in the city her whole life! The counters were loaded with containers filled with milk! We thought we found a solution to that problem. We would get a pig to fatten on the extra milk and cream.

One Sunday afternoon while the boys were napping, we decided to walk around our property. I was accustomed to a small city lot, not sixty five acres of land! We could see the fence line on the south from the bay window in the dining room. That was the pasture we kept Dolly cow in. We hiked up the back hill into the woods to the property line on the west. The northern border was a stone fence about four feet high. We were amazed about all the work that must have gone into clearing the land of rocks and erecting that wall. On the other side of the wall was a corn field. "Wouldn't fresh corn taste good for supper?" I climbed over the wall and began to select a few ears when I heard a rustling noise; someone was coming through the corn field. I quickly hopped over the fence and tucked the ears of corn next to the wall so they wouldn't be seen.

My Mother had always said to me, "If I don't catch you, God will". Well, God did not appear. Rather it was two men, one elderly and the other in his late 20's, about George's age. They asked if we had seen any heifers. "Heifers", I said, "What are heifers?" The two bent over with laughter. Of course they recognized a young, ignorant, city girl when they met one. We introduced each other and on parting the older man said, "This is cow corn. Come down to the house and I'll give you all the sweet corn you can eat." That began our friendship with the Hibbards. The father was called Hibbie and the son was Gordon. Gordon was a veteran returned from the South Pacific theatre of war.

We would never have lasted on that farm without the Hibbard Family. They helped us, advised us and took care of us. They found us the pig to drink the extra milk. The pig was put in a small pen attached to the outside of the barn. It was my responsibility to slop the pig. George had started his teaching position in Endwell. We would get up early enough to milk Dolly and get George off to work for nearly an hour's commute. Then I would get the little boys up. Later in the day, usually while the boys napped, I would feed the pig and clean up the barn. Unfortunately, we had to buy pig feed. Milk alone was not sufficient. The worst part was chasing that pig back into its pen when it would root out under the wire of the pen. One day I had raked up the dropped apples from under the crabapple tree. I dumped them into the pig's trough. He ate them with gusto. Later, when I went to feed him he was weaving on his feet and had a silly grin on his face. He was drunk! The rotted, fermented apples did it.

By late fall, the pig had filled out enough (he was now fat) to be slaughtered. Hibbie did the honors. With knife in hand he jumped onto the pig's back and slit his throat. I shall never forget the blood-curdling squeal that pig gave out! Now the pig had to be shaved. A big barrel filled with water was heated from below with a good hot fire. The pig was moved by block and tackle and dunked in the boiling water to soften the bristles. The men; Gordon, Hibbie and George removed the hairs with scrapers. Next the animal was gutted and ready to take to the butcher in town where it was cut up, packaged and frozen and placed in a frozen locker for which we paid monthly rent. The hams were sent away to be smoked for a nominal fee. By the time the meat reached our table it had cost a small fortune.

With cold weather approaching, we had to think of fuel for heat. George had been a camper and knew about gathering wood to burn. Now he had to use those skills to get heat for our house. I was his assistant. While the boys napped we accomplished a lot. We would ride the iron-wheeled tractor to the woods and cut down a tree that George would have chosen before hand. With a two-man saw we would cut down a good sized tree. He was on one handle of the saw and I held the other end. That was really hard work. He would drag the log to the saw table with the tractor and after sawing it length-wise, cut it into chunks to fit in the wood stove. That became our Sunday afternoon entertainment all fall. When it got too cold and snowy we had to order coal for delivery. Since we had no coal bin in the cellar, the coal was dumped under the roof over the ramp to the barn's second story. As a result we had to carry buckets of coal to feed the furnace throughout the winter.

Farmhouse in Triangle, New York 1946

Winter arrived, changing the scene to a wonderland. There was deep, white snow everywhere. The trees bent over with their heavy loads. George skied down the back hill while the boys and I rode on a sled. The Hibbards hitched up a horse to a wagon that had runners and we all went for a ride in the crisp, clear air. I vividly recall one moonlit night. It was bitter cold. Looking out the bay window we could see wild rabbits hopping on the deep snow. The moon was so bright we could clearly see the rabbits as they played.

Just before Christmas, the Hibbards told us that Dolly cow was going to freshen. Oh! Yet, another new word in my vocabulary. To freshen meant the cow would soon have a calf which would bring on a fresh supply of milk. They told us not to milk her until the calf was born. Good, that was one less task to do, although I still had to clean out the box stall each day. On a below zero morning, February 3, I went to the barn to feed Dolly and there stood a calf. "Oh, Dolly," I said, "You've just had a baby!" As she moved I could see something hanging from the back of her. I became upset thinking she had pushed so hard to bring out the baby that she was turning inside out. I hurried into the house, grabbed the two boys, bundled them up, put them on the sled and ran the full mile down the road to Hibbards. First thing, Hibbie scolded me for bringing those two babies out in the bitter cold. He hustled them into their warm kitchen near the coal burning stove. Then he and Gordon got in their truck and went to look at Dolly cow. When they returned they were laughing at me for not knowing about afterbirth. How would I know? I was anesthetized before delivering my babies and never knew anything until the next morning when I was presented with a beautiful bundle from heaven. Now Dolly became very difficult for us to milk. She wouldn't stand still and she would kick dangerously. So the Hibbards took her to their barn and milked her with their herd with the milking machines. We just picked up the fresh milk and cream as we needed it from their cooler. That was such a good deal. The owners had their cow boarded, Hibbards had extra milk to send to the creamery and we had a plentiful supply. The calf was a male, so the Hibbards took it to be sold. No more cow for us to tend.

Early, early in the spring we drove to the railroad station in Greene to pick up an order of baby chicks that had arrived. George had prepared a room in the barn with a brooder and feeder. We all adored the fuzzy, peeping little birds. This led to a new farm chore, I had them to feed each day while George was at work.

Meanwhile, up the long driveway came a pair of horses pulling a sleigh with a big tank mounted on it. The sleigh stopped near the woods. Several men got off and began drilling holes in certain trees and pounding in small drains upon which they hung buckets. The boys and I watched for hours as we sat together in the bay window. The next few weeks the sleigh returned almost every day. The men emptied the buckets into the big tank. The Hibbards told us it was another neighbor, Mert, who always sugared off that thicket of maple trees. Next to his barn Mert had a sap house where he boiled down the sap into syrup. Someone had to keep those fires going day and night and watch for the correct time to drain off the syrup while making sure it didn't burn. For using our trees Mert gave us three gallons of wonderful sweet syrup.

Springtime brought new tasks. The garden had to be spaded. Both George and I worked at that. The sod was turned over and ready to be loosened. The baby chicks were pretty well grown by now but still remained in the barn at night. During the day I would let them out to scratch in the newly dug garden to break up the clods of earth. They did a very good job.

As Memorial Day approached we made plans to visit family out of town. I was to have things packed and ready to leave as soon as George arrived home from school, which I did. I had bathed the two boys and put them down for their naps. When I took my bath, a cloudburst hit. Driving rain was pounding the windows when I happened to think about those young chickens. They would drown or catch cold. I had to rescue them. I started to put on rain gear when I thought "You're already wet, why bother?" So out I went naked as the day I was born and put the chickens back in the barn. They were saved. Returning to the house I finished preparations for our holiday. The storm passed as suddenly as it began. George arrived, loaded the car and off we went.

Summer was pleasant. George was home most of the time. He enjoyed his time with the little boys and me. He also did a good bit of fly-fishing in the nearby Geneganslet River.

67

We needed to finish off the second floor of the house. The boys were growing and needed their own room. We made a deal with a lumbering company. They would log the woods on our property in exchange for the needed material to complete the rooms upstairs. A carpenter was hired and the work begun. The new floor was put down, partitions were put up, and bath equipment was installed. The lumbering was going on. The upstairs was beginning to take shape. When the wallboard was in place, George and I spent many hours spackling the seams and making them smooth. The day came when we moved upstairs for sleeping.

Meanwhile, the asparagus bed was harvested as was the rhubarb, the red raspberries, the currants and the vegetable garden. The chickens had been moved to the hen houses. The roosters had been killed, eaten or canned. The beans, beets, corn and tomatoes were also canned along with many jars of jelly and jam.

One day, it became noticeable the feathers were getting thinner on the chickens. Some were looking a little bald. We also saw that they had diarrhea. Chicken refuse is usually rather mushy, but this was runny. We decided to kill them all and can them before they got too sick. It's a good thing we didn't become farmers. We couldn't milk the cow, we lost money on the pig meat and now we couldn't even raise healthy chickens.

As summer came to an end so did our money. Teachers were not paid over the summer. We had used a lot of what little reserve we had on completing the rooms upstairs. We needed more income. Our neighbor who lived up the road was expecting her first child so she was let go from working at the telephone company. She offered to watch my two boys for a fee so I could go to work. Good deal. So I began job hunting. There was an opening for a proof reader at a local publishing company. I was perfect for the job, but I was rejected because I was still of child-bearing age. They did not want to train a person and then have her leave. This was the year 1947. My neighbor was let go because she was expecting and I wasn't hired because I was a young woman! There was no such thing as maternity leave or equal rights for women.

I did eventually find work at an insurance company, typing and filing. I rode in and out of Binghamton with George. That extra money was good, but within six months I was pregnant and had to leave. Paul was born July 2, 1948 at the end of our second year on the farm. He was the most beautiful baby and so easy to care for. Always smiling and cooing.

The children were sick more often than I thought they should be. George was bringing home the germs from all the children at school. Our children never saw other children because we lived so isolated. He had to be the carrier. On a house visit that Dr. Rappaport made to tend to Jimmy who was running a high fever, he also looked at Tommy who had mumps. A glance in the bassinette caused him to say, "You sure have your hands full." There lay baby Paul covered with chicken pox! All recovered uneventfully in due time.

Since I was unable to leave the children to seek employment to contribute to the family coffers, George found extra work. He agreed to teach and coach at the Boys Club in Endicott after school and evenings. Then he needed two brown-bagged meals; one for lunch and one for dinner. He left for school at 7 in the morning and returned at 11 at night. It was a long, tiring day for him and a long, lonely day for me. I was very busy but had no one to talk to except the two little boys and a baby who were very happy playing together.

When our third summer approached a stranger knocked on our door. It was a real estate agent. He asked if we were interested in selling. Was I! George and I talked it over.

Housing in the city was now available. The long drive to work would be eliminated. He needed money to return to college to get his master's degree in order to get a permanent teaching certificate. I was expecting our fourth baby. So we agreed to sell. We moved into an apartment in Endicott. George started his master's program.

We purchased our first television set in 1949. This opened a whole new view for all of us. The programming began at noon with a soap opera and ended at midnight with a comedy show. There were programs for children, too. Hop-a-long Cassidy was their favorite. He was dressed in all black with a large cowboy hat and a gun belt holding two guns. To dress and carry guns like Hop-a-long was the only wish they had for Christmas. Christmas morning when we awoke, we were surprised that the boys were not awake. We went into their bedroom and there they were asleep in their beds. The gun holsters and hats were hanging on the bed posts. They had gotten up secretly and ever so quietly in the middle of the night, found their presents from Santa, put them on and returned to bed. They were sleeping in white flannel sheets. Those black cowboy suits looked like they had been in a snowstorm. They were covered in white lint.

A new war was being fought at this time. It was referred to as the Cold War. It involved Russia advancing the spread of Communism. It led to open conflict on the peninsula of Korea. United States Forces backed by the United Nations entered combat in the late spring of 1950. We were not directly affected by the fray since we had no family members called into service.

My Dad had been ill for over two years with cancer. He passed away the day my daughter was born. I was confined to the hospital and was not informed until the funeral was over. Patricia Ann Morris was born on a cold, icy March 13th. At last a girl! When the nurse brought her to me all cleaned up she was wearing a green bow for St. Patrick's Day in her lavish, coal-black curly hair. We had to name her Patricia especially when George and I could not agree on a name. He had insisted it be Jeanette and I was determined it would not be Jeanette. I wanted Susan. Naming her Patricia settled that difference. What a joy to dress and primp a little girl. She was content to be in her colorful, toy-filled playpen where she could watch her brothers from a safe haven. A happy baby, if you didn't pick her up. She filled out quickly. Everyone who held her couldn't resist patting her full, round bottom. She soon learned it wasn't pleasant to be held, especially by strangers.

Jimmy had started school while we were on the farm. He was picked up by bus at 7:30 each morning returning home after 4:30. He would be so tired he would just flop in my arms and sob. It was so much nicer for him to be near enough to walk from home to school and to come home for lunch every day. There were children on the street for my children to play with. It was nice for me, too, to have neighbors.

Morris Family: Jeanette, Jimmy, Patti, George, Tommy, and Paul 1952

George spent the summer completing his Masters Degree at Cortland College fifty miles away. He stayed on campus

71

during the week, returning to the family on the weekend. While at college he was offered a position for one year to fill in for a professor on sabbatical leave. He so wanted to get his foot in the door to teach at the college level, but could not risk being out of work in another year. He declined the offer.

The summer of 1951 George worked full time at the Boys Club. It was not enough money to cover the rent and other expenses. I found work at a day and all night restaurant. I worked from 6 p.m. until 2 a.m. It was busy when I went to work, slowed down for a few hours and became busy again when the movies let out and again when the night spots closed. I made more money in tips than George was paid in salary. He was in charge of the children at night and I cared for them in the daytime. Everyone took a long afternoon nap!

Our next home was a small house we rented on the hill top of Farm-to-Market Road in the outskirts of Endwell. We had a large lot for the children to play and room for a dog house. A beagle hound named Jack soon lived there. George enjoyed training the dog in the fields nearby. They spent many pleasant hours together. Jack became a very good rabbit dog. It wasn't too long before Jack had company. George bought another beagle we named Jenny. George and the boys and the dogs spent most of their free time tramping the fields.

While living on Farm-to-Market Road, Paul started school. Now all the boys were in school. Just Patti and I were at home. I was asked to do some substitute teaching at Hooper School. My friend, Billie, offered to watch Patti while I taught. By now I was thinking about a full time teaching position of my own. I was advised to apply in Binghamton because the superintendent of schools there had the power to give temporary licenses. I made an appointment with him.

The United States was now prospering. The ex-servicemen were now fathers many times over. The population had exploded with what were to be called the Baby Boomers. The schools were crowded and there was a teacher shortage. I met with Superintendent Martin Helfer. He felt I was well qualified to be in the classroom because of my college preparation and my experience with my own children. He granted me a temporary license to teach with the ultimatum to complete my degree studies. I immediately enrolled in two night classes offered by the local Harper College (now called SUNY Binghamton University).

It was October 1954 that I received a call to teach at Roosevelt School in the city of Binghamton, New York. I was told the present third grade teacher was very ill, so I should plan on a long assignment. I arranged with Billie to take Patti, I made an appointment with the principal of the school to see her on Saturday and pick up materials I would need for Monday. I was all set. My send off from that meeting was Hurricane Hazel that ripped through our area over the weekend and caused widespread flooding. Fortunately, by Monday the debris was removed sufficiently to allow my career to get underway.

It took a lot of cooperation on everyone's part for me to delve into the world of work. With just one car, we all climbed in and got going each morning. George was let out first at the new Junior High School that had just been built. The three boys got out at Hooper School. Patti was taken to Billie's. Then on I drove to Binghamton and my school. On the return it was pick up Patti, drive to the Junior High School to get the boys who after school were taken by the school bus to their Dad who was busy coaching. The three of them stayed in the equipment room in the gym until I came to get them. They were so good and well behaved! They never interrupted the practice session. Onward the car went carrying us home where I began preparing dinner. At 6 o'clock I drove back to the school to get George. We all sat down to dinner and settled in for the evening. It all worked just fine. When a child would become ill, I stayed home with him the first day and George the next. They were seldom ill having already been immunized by their bouts with childhood diseases when they were so young.

Patti was the only one that complained. She did not like staying at Billie's. She missed her mommy. Near the Christmas holiday I had taken her to my school for the Christmas party. She liked going to school and made a plan with Paul. Later that January, she faked going into Billie's house when she got out of the car and instead walked one block to the school where Paul waited for her. He took her to his class room as his guest for the day. He charged her lunch. At the end to of the school day he took her on the school bus with him to their Dad's school.

She was not at Billie's when I came for her. I panicked. I had words with Billie over her not informing me that Patti hadn't arrived at her house. I hurried to the Junior High to see George. He smiled at me and said Patti was right in the equipment room with her brothers. I was so relieved to find her.

I went to my principal the next day and tried to resign. My child came first. She arranged for Patti to stay with a neighbor across from school so she could be near me. That worked out beautifully. Patti and I drove to Binghamton together each morning, I brought my lunch across the street to eat with her. At the end of the day we rode back home together. Everyone was happy once again. When the new semester began, Patti enrolled in the beginning Kindergarten class at my school.

Teaching was fun. I loved children. This was an era when most children were well behaved. There were thirty two third graders in my room. They were delightful. School policy, at least Freda Baudendistal, the school principal's policy, required every teacher to be on her feet if there was even one child still in the room. She monitored us to be sure we were up on our feet. I was in agreement with the policy because it was how teaching should be done. I stayed at Roosevelt School in Binghamton for two years.

Chapter 7
Teaching at Last

The extra pay check, $3,000, I received for my first year of teaching, was most welcome. In no time we caught up with the bills and began to save money for our own house. Many housing developments were being built in Endwell. The IBM Company was expanding very fast. Workers were flooding the area. New houses were going up everywhere. George and the shop teacher visited one site during their lunch hour. That evening George took me to look at the houses being built. It wasn't long before we moved into 3611 Lorne Drive. It was a Cape Cod style with the exact space we desired for our family. The master bedroom was on the main floor. A very large bedroom upstairs was just perfect for the three boys and their three single beds. A cozy smaller room was for our one girl. A second bathroom was located upstairs. Along with a living room, dining room and a kitchen the house was perfect for us. It was located on a south facing hill overlooking Endwell, a view of the Susquehanna River and even across the river to the hills of Vestal. We claimed it to be a million dollar view. We enjoyed living there over twenty five years.

After 10 years it became clear that the floor plan lacked a second doorway into the dining room. The only entrance into the dining room was through the kitchen. Whenever we entertained, guests had to go from the living room, through a short hall, past the master bedroom, past the bathroom, into the kitchen and then into the dining room. This annoyed me to no end. George didn't see it as any problem. During Easter break from school, I emphatically pointed out that there should be a new opening in the wall separating the dining room from the entryway. George was unwilling to cut into the wall out of fear of electrical wiring that could be in the way.

I became exasperated. I went down to the cellar, picked up a

76

hammer, brought it to the site and said, " There should be an opening right here!" BAM!. I drove the hammer deep into the wall. Patti let out a scream and ran to the neighbors, scared that her mother had gone crazy. After picking away the pieces of plaster board we discovered the doorway had already been framed in. We only had to purchase the trim and finish off the opening. At last the dining room was accessible from the living room.

Soon after we moved into our new house a teaching position opened in Westover School which was just a five minute drive from home. I applied for the job and got it. It was a dream position. There even was my very own stapler on my desk! In Binghamton the classes had to share a stapler which was kept in the office. I was jokingly accused of eating staples because I borrowed the stapler so often. Smaller classes and better supplies made my work even more pleasant.

Patti was enrolled in Kindergarten at Hooper School in Endwell in September. The year progressed and she was happy. Then in March she had her sixth birthday. She remarked, "I had a birthday and I was in kindergarten and now I'm having another birthday and I am still in kindergarten!" Having started school in January in my school in Binghamton gave her an extra half year.

The first man-made satellite went into orbit on October 4, 1957. It was launched by the Russians. They had beaten the United States in the race into space. Many feared this was more than a challenge in space. This reflected on our whole educational system as well as our cultural values. Immediately education was affected. Teachers were retrained in math and science which became the core of the curriculum. Scholarships and free courses were offered to teachers. We all had to take more science to upgrade our classroom teaching.

3611 Lorne Drive 1960

Life went along quite smoothly. I continued to take courses to complete my degree. The summer of 1958 I traveled daily to the campus at Cortland and completed my studies and received my Bachelors of Science degree. I was granted my permanent license to teach common branch subjects in New York State. It was just fifteen years later than my original class graduation date of 1943.

Like any profession, teaching had its ups and downs. I was assigned to the third grade. The first week I was visited by Mary Watkins, the fourth grade teacher. She had a tall, red-headed, freckle-faced boy in tow. "Mrs. Morris," she said, "Billy's going to stay with you until he learns to read." What a challenge for me. I knew the Remedial Reading teacher in Endwell so I called her and asked for help. She invited me to bring him to her after school for testing. I did that. The test results proved he knew very little about reading. She suggested I take him right back to the primer and build from there. Well, Billy was twelve years old and taller than me, no way would I make him read those silly stories while the rest of the class could listen. I made a deal with him. If he would not be disruptive in the classroom and was willing to sacrifice gym, art and music classes, I would give up my free preparation time and read with him alone. He agreed. What a wonderful experience for both of us. He was such a fine boy in spite of an alcoholic, abusive family. He became my right hand man in the classroom; cleaning the chalkboard, lining up the other children and keeping the room neat and tidy. I was so proud of our work together. He reached second grade level in that one year. We agreed to meet three times a week during the summer to continue our progress. That boy later graduated from high school. My principal was also impressed with his progress and asked me to become the remedial reading teacher for Westover School.

Now I needed more training in special education. I began the program of study at Syracuse University, 90 miles to the north, in the summer session. I drove to Syracuse every Monday morning taking Patti with me. We stayed with my mother all week driving back to Endwell every Friday afternoon. Meanwhile, George was taking charge of our three boys. They loved it. His summer employment was teaching swimming and life guarding at the IBM Country Club. They got to hang around the clubhouse playing games and swim in the pool every day. Everyone was happy.

Endwell had grown so fast we needed more schools. A new elementary school was built just two blocks down from our house. The school system in the little town of Maine was joined with Endwell and became the centralized school district of Maine-Endwell. A new high school was constructed. George was very involved in the development of the Physical Education and Recreation facilities. He had been promoted as well to Athletic Director. Now with a new high school, an interscholastic athletic program also had to be developed. New teams had to be formed and coaches recruited. The first class to occupy the new school was the

79

tenth grade. The students were too young and small to field a competitive football program so George introduced the area's first soccer team. Other schools followed his lead and soon soccer became very popular in the Binghamton area.

Life was too good to last. By the time I returned to teaching in the fall, I noticed my monthly period had stopped. It must have been the change of life. Upon going to the doctor, I discovered I was once again pregnant! There was no "Pill" in that era. I was so mad! I called George every name in the book. "There was no sense in giving a woman a brain; she is nothing but a body!" George had been able to get his Master's Degree and thirty hours of study in Administration. Having babies didn't slow him down. I had enough children, I didn't need more. However, I was going to have another baby.

I always felt well when pregnant. One relief was you couldn't get pregnant because you already were. I continued teaching until the end of February. During a tremendous snow storm we received word that George's Dad had passed away. The usual two hour drive became six hours of dreadful weather. We stayed with his Mother until after the funeral. One week later, early in the morning, I began to hemorrhage. I roused Jimmy, now sixteen, to take over the other children and get them fed and off to school, George rushed me to the hospital. I was put on complete bed rest and seemed to recover. George's Mother came to take care of the family. Patti, now ten years old, wrote me a loving note with a picture she had drawn of her new baby sister to be.

After three days, I was sent home to more bed rest. Granny Morris took care of the household. She was glad to be busy during her grieving. Two days later the bleeding began again. This time I was kept in the hospital. Dr. Nowicki spent the whole day at my bedside. In the evening when the operating room was empty, Dr. Ness appeared. The two doctors conferred and decided to perform a Caesarian section. I knew I had brought all this on myself and baby because I didn't want another baby. Thankfully, Geoffrey George was born healthy. Patti sent me another note while I was confined in the hospital. It said," I hate you! I hate you! You just borned a boy!"

It was a beautiful spring. I was at home with my new baby. It felt good to be a housewife and mother again. The other children were pretty well grown up. They enjoyed the baby, too. As Geoffrey grew older they all helped in raising him. Granny Morris moved to Endwell and took care of him when I returned to teaching. He always had someone to play a game with him or to read to him. Jim was interested in building model airplanes that hung in his room. Tom was an HO train enthusiast with the tracks, landscapes and buildings taking up most of the cellar. Once, while his grandmother was watching soap operas on TV instead of watching him, Geoffrey went after the suspended model planes with a whiffle ball bat. Jim was so mad.   In those two places Geoffrey was not allowed to be by himself. While the rest of us spoiled him with love and attention the two biggest brothers disciplined him.   In spite of all of us and the attention he grew up well and happy.

It was a breath-taking event in April 1961 as the student body gathered in the auditorium to view the televised first American manned space rocket launch. We all were glued to the set watching as Alan Shepherd rocketed into space. He made it! The United States had succeeded in space.

Each Christmas my Mother chose something for the house as our gift. On one occasion we received a replica of an antique coin glass vase. It was amber colored and attractive. It fit nicely in our Early American décor of the dining room. However, George lifted the vase into the air as if it were a trophy and claimed, "Your mother really loves me!", thus registering his disapproval of a vase for him. The vase found a home in the hutch in the dining room where it held fresh flowers from time to time as the seasons allowed.

Weekends were especially busy for me. I attempted to do a week's work on a weekend as most working mothers did. There was housework, laundry, cooking and baking. I always made a complete dinner for Sunday; a roast, potatoes, gravy, salad, vegetable and dessert. On a Sunday in October when all was ready, I called the family, who were in the den in front of the television set watching NFL football, to come to the table. No one moved or said a word. I repeated myself a bit louder and still no response. Someone piped up with "It's not half-time!"

That did it! I was inflamed! I declared, "I'm leaving! I must be some kind of fool to work so hard taking care of the house and family and turning every penny of my salary from teaching school over to the family coffers for the privilege of waiting on all of you! Well, I can live very well supporting just myself alone!" I turned on my heel to leave when George dashed into the dining room, picked up the replica of the antique coin glass vase and handed it to me saying, "Be sure you take this with you." That defused me. I began laughing. I thought he was so clever and funny.

The next decade moved along quickly as the family matured. We were school centered and sports participants. In the mid 1960's the world was changing radically. Everything seemed to be moving faster and louder. New communities were springing up in the suburbs. Good jobs were looking for people to fill them. New music filled the air. Elvis and the English exports, the Beatles, influenced everything. Recreational and experimental drug use became common. The style of dress changed the look of the youth; long hair, tight fitting, pegged trousers and pointed shoes were "in". Our family was affected very little by this atmosphere.

Jim and Tom could always find their own things to do. They carried papers on a paper route to earn spending money.

They were good hard working boys. Then, late one summer they investigated a bulldozer that stood idle in the hills near a new upscale development nearby. They were not the only visitors to the bulldozer. Children aged five and up, had climbed around and over the abandoned equipment for weeks. However, the Morris boys and their friends, having discovered a tool box on the machine, over a period of days began dismantling what they could loosen and remove. They were observed by a workman from the project. The developers complained to the police.

It wasn't long before we received a visitor from the State Police. Tom's eyes opened as big as saucers when he saw the gun strapped on the uniform of the Trooper. He told in detail everything they had done. Two months later we ended up in family court along with the parents and sons of the other miscreants. The judge was very fair. When the developers wanted us to pay to replace that bulldozer that was not in working order and was an enticement for all the neighboring children, he was turned down. Since the boys had been truthful and cooperative, they were dismissed after listening to a beneficial lecture from the judge. Whew!

Both of the older boys swam on the swim team and ran on the track team in season as the new high school developed teams. George was the coach of the successful track team and also the coach of the basketball team even though he had been promoted to Athletic Director for the nine schools in the Maine Endwell District. I spent many hours cheering for all of them.

I was then a full time Remedial Reading teacher. The little Westover School had been swallowed up by the Johnson City School District in a consolidation. The Superintendent assigned me to Oakdale School as well as Westover. That worked quite well.

The summer of 1964 found the family basking in the sun on

the sandy New Jersey shore at Wildwood. We had just delivered our second son Tom to Kings Point, where he had gained a congressional appointment to the United States Merchant Marine Academy to study marine engineering. After attending the swearing in ceremony, we continued our journey to include a short vacation at the shore.

Our teenager Paul asked to go on a deep sea fishing trip. We chose a half-day excursion for the afternoon. Never having been out on the ocean, we were excited as we boarded. George, Paul, and Patti were to fish while I kept watch of young Geoffrey to be sure he was safe and not annoying the other passengers.

I found myself a sunny spot on deck where I could soak up the rays while I attended to Geoff. Wearing bright yellow short shorts and a halter top, I was ready for some serious sun tanning. The powerful engines throbbed and the water splashed as we cut a path out to sea. Everyone was in high spirits while looking forward to a fine catch.

When we arrived at the fishing grounds, the captain cut the engines. We were now adrift wallowing in the waves. The boat began to sway from side to side and up and down as the sea swells rocked the boat heavily. I soon began to feel queasy. I scrambled to my feet and found George who had already begun fishing over the side of the boat. I told him I was sick and was afraid I would vomit. He suggested I go to the other side of the boat when I got sick so I would not disrupt his fishing.

I went to the other side and leaned far over the rail as best as I could to avoid messing up the deck. I was so sea sick. Where was Geoffrey? I didn't know and I didn't care! While hanging over the railing, the captain of the boat came over to me and said, "Mother, do you want to buy this boat?"

"Why should I?" was my response.

"If you buy the boat, you can order me to take you to shore."

Somehow, I endured the remainder of the fishing expedition, Some fish were caught, but no whoppers. Mine was the only fish story worth retelling. Once on shore, I regained by equilibrium and we went on to dinner.

The end of the 1964 school year was a fractious time for our third son. Paul marched or should I say danced, to a different drummer. He was more social, loved the girls and desired the latest fashion. (Sounds like his mother.) When his academic marks faltered, we offered to send him to a private military school where he would be away from poor influences, as well as free from his domineering parents. He readily agreed. The school required prepayment in full. Our coffers were not that full. I borrowed the money from the bank in exchange for my paycheck every month for a year. It was a sound investment. Our home became more peaceful without the disagreements. More importantly he completed his high school with a high standing and was accepted at college.

Chapter 8
Tanzania 1966

The following year the Superintendent wanted to add another school to my duties. I balked saying it would be just "lip service" to be spread so thin. I asked to be returned to the classroom where I could see progress. Instead of taking that assignment, I accompanied George to Tanzania in East Africa where he had volunteered to teach.

The New York State Teachers' Association published a monthly magazine which was sent to every teacher in the state. In that magazine was an article about a teacher working in East Africa. At dinner I asked George if he had read that article. He had. We entered into a conversation wondering what the opportunities would offer. Patti, now sixteen, ridiculed us for thinking we would go to Africa when we hadn't been able to take an often desired trip to Maine. Her scoffing led to George writing a letter of inquiry. Six months later after the paper work was completed, psychological testing done and personal interviews held, we found ourselves at Columbia University for the summer studying the language and customs of the people of East Africa.

The "we" I refer to includes sixteen year old Patti and six year old Geoffrey. Jim had enlisted in the Navy when the Vietnam draft had called him after completing a year of college. Tom was a student at the Merchant Marine Academy and Paul was to attend college at Cortland. The two younger boys, now 20 and 18, stayed in our house in Endwell and had summer jobs.

The program was titled Teachers' for East Africa, TEA. Sponsored by the State Department as aid to developing countries, it was administered by Columbia University. Interviews were held in New York City, Chicago, Miami and San Francisco. George and I were psychologically tested and interviewed at Columbia early in the spring. Those selected were brought to Columbia for orientation and assignments. The program included the countries of Kenya, Uganda and Tanzania. From the beginning George had insisted that he remain in his field of Physical Education. He was convinced that the lessons learned in sports activities such as; teamwork, leadership, cooperation were necessary for the future leaders of the developing country. He also was to teach health, another necessary field of knowledge.

We had sub-leased an apartment in New York City for the summer semester at Columbia University where all four of us attended classes. That was culture shock. We were on the fifth floor of an apartment building with our windows facing the law college where every light blazed the entire night. The sounds of traffic, sirens and ambulances filled the air. It was hot and stifling and noisy with construction going on all day. As soon as classes were over each Friday afternoon we headed back to the peace and quiet of our Endwell home. There I would take care of the laundry and cleaning and prepare a couple of casseroles for Tom and Paul for the week.

George and I were enrolled in classes to learn the history, culture and language of East Africa. The children only took language classes. The studies were an awakening to a whole new culture, far different than what we experienced. While in New York City, when time permitted we would walk around town mingling with the crowds and feeling the energy of the city. We also took in a few plays on Broadway. Friends from Endwell took advantage of free housing and came to visit with their children to see the sights. The summer went very quickly.

By the end of August, we were ready to depart for our assignment. Each of us had endured the many preventative shots that were required to protect us from endemic diseases. Our furniture at home was stored and the house rented for two years. The boys would not be staying there while in college. They had both grandmothers and many aunts and uncles with whom they could stay for holidays and vacations. The recommended list of items to be sent ahead in crates of sea freight was on its way. We were ready for an adventure.

The Saturday before departure, I began to have difficulty swallowing. Saliva was building up in my mouth. I went to the doctor. He gave me a prescription that would calm my nerves. I did not know I was that worried or concerned over leaving my life as I knew it, for a life in the unknown and unfamiliar. With the pills I recovered and we boarded the plane along with fifty other families.

The plane landed in Dakar, Senegal for refueling. We observed soldiers carrying rifles guarding the airport. We did not deplane although it would have been good to stretch our legs after that long flight. It was a frightening sight. We traveled on to Mombasa, Kenya where the teachers and families assigned to that country deplaned. Continuing through the night, we landed in Dar es Salaam, Tanzania. After being helped through customs by the Ministry of Education representative, we were bussed to the hotel. All of this happened at night. We had seen nothing of our surroundings; everything was pitch black from the airport to the hotel where we were to stay.

I awoke early to the bustling sounds of morning. I stepped out on the balcony of our room and drank in the sights and smells. Palm trees were wafting in the gentle breeze. The Indian Ocean lapped against the shore to the east. The modern building of the Barkley's Bank was directly across from me. To the left was the clock tower on a church building announcing meridian time and Swahili time which began at one o'clock each day when the sun rose. There were few vehicles other than bicycles. People were going hither and thither. Some of them were dressed in neat western clothing. Others wore the long white tunic and turban of the Sikhs. Most of the women were wrapped in brightly colored fabrics over their simple dresses. The women carried loaded baskets on their heads. I felt as if I were in a picture from a National Geographic magazine.

A knock on the door brought me back into the room. It was the servant bringing tea, their custom is to "knock you up and serve tea" early in the morning. Breakfast was served buffet style downstairs near the lobby. So many different foods, fruits and breads, covered with yards of cheese cloth to keep out the flies. Nothing appealed to me. The sight of so many flies blackening the protective cloths killed my appetite. The rest of the family found suitable food. I went many days refusing the food. We located an import store that sold a jar of peanut butter and a box of crackers that I was able to eat.

The next few days were busy preparing for the road trip to the assigned school. The group, the fifteen who were assigned to Tanzania, spent time at the Ministry of Education getting assignments and instructions. We were invited to the home of another TEA teacher who had completed one of the two years of his assignment. He had a lovely home with a cashew tree growing in his yard. I enjoyed the American food refreshments that were served. We needed to purchase a car. We were able to find a new Volkswagen station wagon. We took an afternoon dip in the salty Indian Ocean. We were entertained at the American Embassy. It was a busy week.

The assignment given to George and Gene Hanson (from southern California) was to go to the mission school at Peramiho five hundred miles away in the bush. Gene was to teach Science and George was given the subject of English, much to his displeasure. The two families made plans to travel together for safety over the rough roads. The Hansons had purchased a Volkswagen minibus for their family of five, a wife, a son, and two teen-aged girls. The adults had

International Driver's Licenses having acquired them before leaving New York City. Driving on the left seemed strange. The nine of us began our journey into the heart of Africa. We soon learned the pavement ended a few miles outside of town. Packed red dirt was the surface of the road. It didn't take long to realize we had to leave space between the vehicles to let the dust settle and restore visibility. If the rear car approached the lead car red dust coated everything, choked your throat and reduced visibility to zero. There were very few villages along the way. That night we arrived at Iringa where there was a modern motel and restaurant operated by Greek people. It was a pleasant stay.

We continued our journey the next morning. Yet we did not reach Peramiho. By late afternoon we were in need of gas. No gas was available. A native directed us to a mission up in the hills where we were able to get gas. We were invited to spend the night as there would be no place for us to get lodging that far into the bush. The men and boys stayed with the Fathers and the women and girls stayed in the nuns' quarters. They fed us soup and bread for dinner and for breakfast hard, cold blood sausage and hard-cooked eggs along with hot tea. George placed the same amount of money that we had paid in the motel the night before under his plate before we left. Surprisingly, it was very cold in the highlands. A frost was on the ground and the mission was worried about the blossoms on their pear trees. We were south of the Equator so in August they were entering spring.

By afternoon of the next day we arrived at our destination. The mission at Peramiho could be seen from far away. Surrounded completely by a red brick wall, the many buildings, also made of red brick rose above the wall. It looked like the picture of a 17th century Renaissance village in a history textbook. A most impressive cathedral stood in the center. We learned later that during the war all the German priests and missionaries were isolated far back into the bush where they could not be any part of a subversive plot. While there, these industrious people organized and trained the natives and built these beautiful sturdy brick structures.

Father Gerhardt was informed of our arrival and came out to greet us. He had expected two men to teach in their Teacher Training School. He was flabbergasted when he saw two families totaling nine people. Where was he going to put all of us? The nuns took us in for teatime while the Father found accommodations for us. Since the German surgeon was on holiday back in Germany there could be no operations. That left one wing of the hospital empty. That is where he housed us. He located a cook and a house girl to take care of us.

Now that we were temporarily housed what was there for the women and children to do all day every day? There was no cooking, cleaning or laundry to do. Of course, the two men went to the college buildings to teach. There was an elementary school where the young Hanson boy enrolled. Geoffrey started in the first grade class but didn't stay very long. The school children had never seen a white child. Geoffrey was very white, light skinned and hair so blonde it looked white and it was silky. The children began to touch him and stroke his shiny hair. He began to cry. The Headmaster of the school brought him to me. I explained to Geoffrey how interesting he was to the other children just as he had been interested in the black boy that came into the store back home. The following day he tried school again and lasted until lunch time when each child had to wash from the same water bucket. Again he was brought to me. He no longer wanted to try school there. "You are a teacher, Mommy," he said, "You teach me." So I began home teaching. We had no textbooks; we made up stories to read. We counted and added whatever we could. He was such a quick learner, we scrambled for learning opportunities. Within the month our air freight arrived. In it were text books and art materials I had packed before leaving the States. We

91

settled into a schedule of study which solved his problem of schooling.

Meanwhile we also had three teen aged girls with no school to attend. They took long walks around the mission each day. There was much to see. Peramiho was built like a medieval town. There was a bank, a printing shop, a Volkswagen garage, the primary school, the teachers' college, dormitories for the college students, the hospital and several different kinds of houses for those who worked and lived there. In the center of the complex stood a huge cathedral. Outside of the walls were the farms where food was grown. The White Fathers out of Germany had developed and ran this mission.

Peramiho mission cathedral

Father Gerhardt wanted all the personnel he could get that would assist him in his life's work. That is why he welcomed the assistance of the TEA program. The problem we presented to the Tanzanian government was the conflict of church and state. George and Mr. Hanson were recruited by the government and were sent to the mission. The government would not build houses on mission property and the mission would not build for government employees. When three months had passed and the impasse continued, the two men were reassigned by the Administration of Education in Dar es Salaam.   Mr. Hanson was sent to Marangu and George was to teach at Morogoro.

Knowing this would be a two-day drive, George located a large gas container to fill and carry with us. Experience does teach lessons. On the trip back north we did not have the constant fear of being stranded without gasoline.   Petrol stations were few and far between and supplies were very uncertain.

Morogoro was also a mission of the White Fathers of Germany. It had very modern buildings for classrooms and dormitories. There was a small house waiting for us. Now with a home to set up we needed the bedding, dishes, cooking utensils and the other belongings we were advised to send ahead in sea freight. However, after three months our belongings had still not arrived. Nonetheless we set up housekeeping. There were three other American families on the TEA program at this location. They were on the second year of their assignment. They welcomed us and gave us much help in settling in.

Christmas of 1966 was one of the saddest days of my life. While friends and family were getting together and sharing in New York, here we were thousands of miles away from the rest of our family. With heavy hearts we tried to make the holiday somewhat festive but we sadly failed. In order to have a Christmas tree Patti, Geoff and I cut and pasted green construction paper into a tree form. We taped it to a bare wall and added ornaments cut from colored construction paper that I had included in the sea freight. Santa brought Geoff a small native drum and a Monopoly game with the theme of London streets, the best he could do. What a sad, heart-aching day that was. The next day we drove to Nairobi, Kenya to get Patti ready for school.

Nairobi High School was the only school in all of East Africa for a teen-aged expatriot girl. She had to complete and pass an entrance examination in order to be enrolled. She could have selected a boarding school in Israel or Switzerland, but she didn't want to be so far away from us. Even so, Nairobi was an over five hundred mile distance to travel.

Nairobi was a large, modern city. There we saw beautiful mosques with glistening onion-shaped domes. A large structure displaying a huge cross housed a Lutheran Church. We visited the sprawling campus of Nairobi High School, met the Head Mistress and checked out the dormitories.

A designated tailor shop and store made the school uniforms for her school and other private schools in the area. She was fitted for her gray wool skirt and jacket. We then purchased a gray sweater, several standard white blouses, ankle socks and the red and black striped school tie. The oxford shoes were sold in an annex across the alley from the main establishment. She returned from trying on shoes quite agitated. At the first opportunity, she let the young nice-looking Asian clerk have it with a slap across the face that could be heard throughout the store. No one uttered a sound. The bill was totaled, George paid it and we left the store. Immediately we asked, "What was that all about?" She explained he got "fresh" with her in the shoe store. Since she was alone there with him, she waited until she was safely with others to get even. "He'll think twice before touching another American girl," she declared.

Her classes would begin in mid-January. Before leaving Kenya we spent a day at the Game Park just outside the city watching wild animals roam their natural habitat. A story was told by our guide about a lion running loose in the city of Nairobi frightening everyone until he was caught and returned to the wild.

We stayed in the home of another TEA teacher while in Nairobi. On the way back to our home in Tanzania, we stopped to visit the Hansons who were then living in Marangu near Mt. Kilimanjaro. We celebrated New Years Eve with them. Chella and the girls put on quite a spread considering the limited availability of groceries. They served chicken salad in cream puff shells. Delicious. New Years Day 1967 found us climbing the famous snow-capped volcano. We hiked to the first rest shelter which was at the height of nearly 10,000 feet. It was a gentle climb having begun from the parking area which was already 5,000 feet above sea level. The mountain has two peaks; Mawenzi and Kibo which are snow-covered all year in spite of setting just south of the Equator. The peaks are connected by an area called the saddle. It's a three-day climb to reach the summit. Such ventures are led by guides who are well-acquainted with the mountain and its weather.

Mount Kilimanjaro from Marangu 1967

We thought George, with this teaching assignment in his field of Health, Physical Education and Recreation and the family set up in a house, we would spend the rest of the two years here in Morogoro at the base of the beautiful Uluguru Mountains. The climate was cool and the housing comfortable. There was a nice community of Americans, Canadians and Europeans. Not so. The Education Department informed him to report at Mwanza to a government college. Again the problem of a government worker employed at a church mission. Once again, the conflict of church and state.

We were to travel during the rainy season when the roads often wash out and become unsafe, so we were sent by train to Mwanza, a town located on the northern border of Tanzania along Lake Victoria. We had initially been to the southern and western borders at Peramiho, traveling to Lake Nyasa, next to the eastern mountainous area at Morogoro, and now we were sent north. After packing all of our household and personal belongings again, we boarded the train. Even our car was riding the train. We traveled for two days, spending one night on the train. The government gave us first class accommodations. We were picked up at the station in Mwanza by fellow TEA teachers whom we knew from our classes at Columbia University. They drove us to their residence which was next to the house allocated to us. Burt and Elaine, of Spring Valley, NY, insisted we stay with them until our house was ready for occupancy. The Caplans had two sons, Jessie and Louis. Our Geoffrey was just between the two of them in age. Life became easier from then on.

The next morning the veranda of our house was full of African men. The news of new Americans had spread ahead of our arrival. The men were looking for work. It was

96

expected that the teachers would hire help. We did have a houseboy at Morogoro. His English was poorer than our meager Swahili. I was determined to find a houseboy with whom I could communicate. I chose Bartholomew. Bartholomew chose his nephew to be the shamba (gardener) boy. He was called Noeli. I immediately had them scrub everything and air all the cushions and mattresses. It was clean and fresh when we moved in having been newly painted throughout by the prisoners who resided at the prison located not far from the college property.

It was a comfortable house with three bedrooms, one bathroom, a dining/living area and the kitchen with a "cooker" (a stove). We purchased a small refrigerator and a device to filter the water after it had been boiled. I found some fabric to cover the cushions of the furniture and to sew draperies for the windows. Native-woven pombe baskets (beer strainers) made attractive shades for the bare light bulbs on the walls. The house became home.

In the rear of the property was housing for the servants. The servant's quarter was a two-room house with a shower bath and a patio. All of the buildings in the compound were made of white stucco. Bartholomew brought his wife, Mary, and his year old daughter, Estha, to his quarters. Bartholomew had been trained by English ex-patriots that had enjoyed good living while living abroad in Mwanza. He was disappointed in our possessions; Melmac dinnerware and no sterling silver to set a proper table. Our instructions for sea freight listed what to pack stressing simplicity. How was I to know we would have a servant who really knew how to entertain?

Bartholomew also gave us his work schedule. It began by serving Memsahib and Bwana tea in their bedroom at 6 a.m. I changed that right away. No tea in bed, breakfast at 7 a.m in the dining room was my plan.

Mwanza house living room 1967

We were thoroughly enjoying our stay in Africa. George was teaching classes and coaching basketball and track. He was competent in his work. There were two other Americans on the staff from the TEA program; Jack from Indiana who taught science and John from Texas in the English Department. John and son Aden from England and a Canadian family with four young children completed our housing compound. We learned of the private school, Isamilo, staffed by Anglicans, that Geoffrey could attend.

Four American young men living on the shore of a lake needed a boat, so George, Burt, John, and Jack hired a row boat made for them. It took about a month to complete the vessel. It was just a small boat that could hold no more than five or six at a time. They named it Teacup for the TEA program. A teacup it turned out to be. It could not be steered by rowing alone. Someone had to steer from the back with the blade of an oar used as a rudder to stay on coarse. Many happy hours were spent paddling around the many islands of Lake Victoria.

Teacup on a fishing trip

One small island was named Sanane where animals roamed in an uncaged zoo. We would row from the mainland to the island in Teacup. It became the place to take out of town guests when they came to visit us.

We walked and climbed among the rocks to catch sight of a tall, gangly reticulated giraffe, a strutting peacock with its tail fanned out exposing irradiant blue-green eyes, a pesky small antelope called a dik-dik or a young inquisitive elephant sniffing through our lunch basket. An attendant with a prod kept the creatures from annoying the visitors too much.

Sanane Island zoo

The lake and other waters were unsafe for swimming. A fluke, Bilharzias, endemic to East African lakes, caused much illness usually by affecting the liver. To swim we had to join the old British country club on the other side of town. It was not very fancy. A building housing a bar and a dance floor had an outdoor pool with a large cistern where the water was purified. The large white stucco wall surrounding the pool was the screen for showing old movies on Sunday nights. We watched Shirley McLain movies and also "Those Amazing Men in their Flying Machines"

I soon learned how to shop for food. An Indian merchant, Karim had an import store where one could purchase canned goods at an exorbitant price. The lake boat came in every other Thursday. I would get fresh eggs and pasteurized milk from there. The meat came from the Lake Butchery. Early each morning a cow was slaughtered, cut up and put on the counter for purchase. With no refrigeration, it was wise to shop early before too many flies contaminated the meat. I would take the filet and the liver. They would still be warm. Care had to be taken to get vegetables because animal excrement was used for fertilizer. Every leaf of lettuce had to be washed with soap and water before it could be eaten. We asked our friends back home to send us packets of seeds and soon we had our own vegetable garden. The large open market was where we purchased bananas, mangos, papaya, potatoes and onions. Live chickens were also for sale. Hand woven baskets, mats and carved bowls as well as fabric from Red China could be bought very cheaply.

Mwanza market 1967

It wasn't long before I was asked to be a part of the education program. The School Leaving Exams needed to be graded. At the end of standard (grade) eight a comprehensive test was given to the students. The top ten percent of the test takers were offered the opportunity to go to the government sponsored and funded secondary schools. The test was named the School Leaving Exam. For the remaining 90 percent of the students, their education was now over. This was such an important exam; it could not be left in the hands of the local educators to mark them fairly and honestly. I was hired along with ten others, mostly ex-patriots, to do the grading of the tests. We reported to the local government building where we were locked in a room while we worked. When I challenged the need of such tight security, I was given the answer that it was necessary because there was an American in the group and Americans shoot their President.

It was a poor time to be an American abroad. We were looked upon as rich, gun-toting and sex-crazed individuals using our money to overpower the world. I was even told by

101

an English wife, "God forbid I should ever have to live in that lawless country." Even if George and I, as well as the other members of the TEA program, didn't accomplish a great deal in raising the quality of education in East Africa, I know we improved the image of Americans. Living and working side by side with the natives we built many friendships and respect for one another.

When the exams were graded and results tallied, I was asked to take over the teaching of English at a government Secondary School. There had been no teacher in that position for three months after the Peace Corps volunteer had left. Bwiru Boys School was eight miles from our residence. Since George could walk to the college campus to where he worked, I drove the car to Bwiru. What a stir I made. In the first place I was the only female on the whole campus and I even dared to drive a car. I made other changes, too. I wanted to change their learning from rote memorization to meaningful usage.

I was assigned to a class of forty four young men aged from fifteen to twenty something. The grade level was Standard II or sophomore in High School. They were very well behaved and courteous. The students sat in their classroom and the teacher came to them from the large faculty room where each teacher had a desk. A student always escorted the teacher carrying her supplies. During the times when they had no teacher, they memorized their texts. I think they knew more rules of grammar than I, but only to recite them instead of applying them. We soon changed all that. Instead of having them copying from their texts, I had them draw pictures showing the action, description and characters. I also played games with them to practice vocabulary. The Swahili language is simple; one word can stand for many things. For example, mkono means arm and any part thereof; shoulder, elbow, wrist or fingers. I would call out a word in English like elbow and they would touch the place on their bodies. They enjoyed that kind of learning. When they got pretty good at it, I would touch the wrong place on my body. That would mix them up and made them really think instead of just copying. We did a lot of oral reading, too, smoothing out the expression and phrasing.

Biwiru Boy's School

The headmaster wanted to hold an Open House for the parents and community. Since I was the only woman on campus, I was designated the hostess who was to provide the refreshments. I baked and baked cookies at home. We were able to buy flour, sugar and spices. No chocolate chips, however. I brought a sheet from home to use as a table cloth and cut some flowers from our garden for a centerpiece. I had already chosen some of my students to assist me in keeping the tea ready and the serving dishes filled. The table looked very nice.

The community responded and many came. When they discovered the refreshments they stopped, ignoring the rest of the displays of the students' work. I had to remove the cookies from their serving dishes and just spread them on

103

the table because the guests just lifted the whole plateful for themselves. They seemed to use more sugar and milk in their tea than tea. My assistants were very busy with refilling of the sugar and the milk. The day was successful, I guess.

October 5, 1967 marked our 25th wedding anniversary. We planned a celebration with an open-house party. Preparing refreshments was a challenge. There was no super-market from which to buy cream cheese to make hors d'oeuves or a relish to purchase. Karim's Import Store stocked flour, sugar, yeast, and eggs, as well as the punch bowls, ladles, cups, and whiskey. I baked cakes, cookies, small pizzas, samosas and chippati to serve. Two bowls of punch, one with spirits and one without were ready.

Our guests were international. Some were teachers at the college and others were United Nations advisors for projects like water supply and electricity production. They hailed from Tanzania, Kenya, England, Czechoslovakia, Israel, Canada, India, and the United States. Many religions were represented such as Islam, Buddhism, Roman Catholic, Baptist, Mennonite, and Methodist. Some guests could not eat meat, some could not imbibe alcohol, and some were trying to diet. They were a colorful group in Uhuru shirts, saris, Muslim tunics, western business suits or casual attire. The celebration was a huge success. We were glad they all spoke English, making conversation among such a diverse group possible.

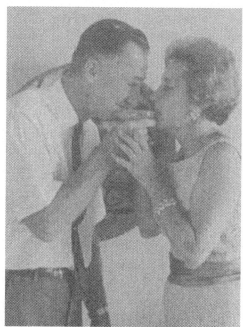
25th Wedding anniversary

The community where we lived housed families of several different nationalities. We carpooled taking the children to Isamilo School. Isamilo was on the way to my school so I drove the children to school in the morning. There were three Africans, one Englishman, three Americans and three Canadians who all climbed in the station wagon. One morning, as I made a right turn off Makingoro Road, a car struck us on the right rear fender. Tanzanians drive on the left side of the road. No one was hurt, but the fender was badly damaged. Another mother who was driving to the school stopped and took my load of children with her. The man who had run into my car was named Saidi. We exchanged information of our insurers. Then I went on my way to school.

Of course, I was late. I explained the accident to the headmaster. He had me call the police station on the phone. It was arranged for me to come in at tea time to file an accident report. When I arrived I was told the report had been made by Saidi and the line had been drawn in the book, so it was finished. I could add nothing. The report was written in Swahili to the effect that I had hit his car.

That evening after school, I took the car to the garage for an estimate for repairs. The Asian who owned the garage expressed his concern over my problem. He thought someone who was in the country to help the people should be treated with more consideration. He contacted the chief of police who agreed to talk with me. The police chief was a huge African wearing his police uniform with many medals decorating his chest. He apologized to me for the poor service and said he would look into the case. He did. As a result a few days later a subpoena was delivered to me at my home by two policemen. I was charged with reckless driving and speeding.

What was I to do? George was away supervising student teachers in the bush country. I had made friends with an Asian woman who owned a beauty parlor. I went to her. She put me in touch with a lawyer. He was not interested in the facts of the incident. We went to court on three different dates only to have my lawyer get a postponement. Finally, the case was heard. The judge declared it poor police work and closed the case. It was then I found out that my lawyer was waiting for a change of circuit judge in order to get a fair judge to hear the case. Bribing officials was a way of doing business. The former judge had been around for too long to be an unbiased arbitrator. Our car insurance paid for the repairs on our car. Saidi didn't get a settlement against me.

George had a run in with the law as well. He had taken the track team to Dar es Salaam for the national finals. While there, he was looking for a little duka, as the stores were called, to buy a package of cigarettes. He was arrested by armed soldiers for carrying a camera while walking past their military training area. In spite of assuring the guards that he

106

had taken no pictures, they confiscated his camera and developed the film. Upon discovering that only pictures of the track meet were on the camera and none of the military installation, the officer in charge asked George why he did not resist arrest. Dumbstruck, George mentioned he came quietly because the soldiers had been pointing machine guns at him. They let him go with no additional trouble.

We made friends with a wonderful man. The Canadian family that was in our compound was transferred to Dar es Salaam. Joyce, the mother, worried over Father Moody. It seems he came each Sunday from his mission to serve Mass at the college, after which he went to their house for breakfast. She wondered where he would eat after they were gone. Offhand I said, "We eat breakfast at our house every Sunday." The first Sunday after they had moved a motorcycle driven by a tall, dark haired white robed priest came to our house. We had breakfast. We enjoyed his company and he enjoyed ours as he visited every Sunday after that and many times when it was not Sunday. Whenever he felt lonely or thought we might need company, he would come by. He would bring his record player, records (always Diana Ross and the Supremes) and a bottle of wine.

Father Moody had had a rough life growing up Catholic in an Irish Protestant neighborhood. He actually was stoned on his way to parochial school. For his teen years he was schooled in France. While there, the Nazis invaded and took the boys from his boarding school as prisoners. They were pressed into hard labor. He claimed his faith is what sustained him those long hard years of war. As a result he pursued studies to become a priest. A well-read and well-traveled man, he was an intelligent conversationalist. We discussed family, religion and world conditions. His mantra was the "responsibility of power". We enjoyed many evenings together.

As Christmas once again approached, I was determined to be

more joyful. I was not going to sit at home and feel lonesome for my other boys. Instead, we planned a Safari. Patti was home on school holiday. We packed the car with coolers of food and a supply of petrol and drove to the Serenora Lodge in the Serengeti Plain. The lodge served meals and offered bathroom facilities with showers. The shower was a small tent with a bucket overhead perforated with holes. Hot water was poured into the bucket and you washed very quickly before the bucket emptied. The sleeping rooms were tents out on the plains. We listened to the howls, roars and barks of the many wild animals roaming the plains during the night.

The rainy season had just passed. The grasslands were lush. The migrations had begun. The next day our drive took us through herds of zebras, gnus and water buffalo. We traveled through forty miles of animals. They were more afraid of the car than we were of them. As we would drive nearer to take pictures they would scatter in all directions. The rains had also left puddles and wadis that George was cautious to drive through not knowing the depth of the water. We didn't want to get stuck because it could be days before we would be rescued in the vast landscape. Patti and I would wade through the water in front of the car to determine its depth. If the water was higher than ankle-deep, George would find a way around it. That was exciting, walking barefoot on the Serengeti Plain.

Serengeti Plain 1967

Our safari took us to Ngorongoro Crater, a huge opening in the earth that had been an active volcano. We were not allowed to drive our own vehicle down the steep slopes into the crater. We hired a Landrover and driver to get onto the floor of the crater. There we observed rhinoceros, leopards, jackals and lions. A lioness could be followed by as many as six cubs as she hunted through the deep grass. The male lions that we saw were taking naps. We saw a lion with bloated belly lying next to her kill, a zebra. Nearby a leopard kept watch for her to leave. A jackal waited to get his fill and the buzzards circled overhead biding their time to swoop in and clean up the carcass. We learned the lion would stay on guard until her mate and all of the cubs came and had their fill. We watched as the animals and birds fed. Finally, the remains would be cleaned up by the ants restoring the land to its natural beauty. The Circle of Life, just like the "Lion King".

Our next thrill was at Lake Manyara. A large herd of elephants were slowly making their way down the escarpment to the water. They crossed the dirt road right in front of our little Volkswagon! Geoffrey hid himself behind the front seat begging his father not to drive any closer because each elephant was bigger than our car. We stopped as they peacefully continued on their way, the adults and their young. This area of land was quite wet. The ground was so saturated with water that the lions slept out on the branches of the trees. We drove right beneath them to take their pictures.

Our journey ended in Arusha. The hotel lobby was decorated with many pictures of John Wayne who years ago had starred in the movie "Daktari" that was filmed in the area. The night-watchman "knocked us up" early in the morning so we could get a head start on the day to make it back to Mwanza by evening. That safari was a worthy reward for our sacrifices and tribulations to come to Africa.

Back home in Mwanza we learned that Mary, Bartholomew's wife, was expecting another child. Since they were part of our household, we were responsible for their medical care. I took Mary to the clinic at the mission where Fr. Moody lived and taught. There was a clinic for prenatal care. Her child, Estha, aged two, came with us in the car. Mary had to wait in a long queue to be seen at the clinic. I cared for Estha while we waited. The day came when Mary was ready to deliver. Bartholomew rode with us to the mission hospital. It was a boy and I named him Jonathan. Mary stayed in the mission hospital for three days. I asked Bartholomew if they had clothes to dress the baby to come home. When the answer was no, I hurried to town to the import store and bought a bolt of white flannel and a pretty baby blanket. Returning home I began hemming diapers and sewing baby sacques. All was ready to bring the baby home. He was a beautiful, healthy baby. Mary was nervous trying to put the clothes on the baby. I dressed him and they were very pleased with how he looked. "Asante sana" they said, (Thank you very much).

110

The next day was Sunday. We were still in bed when Bartholomew rapped on the window to ask for help. Mary was hemorrhaging. I hurried out and drove the family to the local doctor. I gave Bartholomew the money to pay the doctor. They went into his office, leaving me with Estha and Jonathan. There was the baby, naked, wrapped in the new blanket that was badly soiled. I was furious. When I got home, Fr. Moody was there for his breakfast. I began to let off steam about the hopelessness of the African. Even when given everything, they were too backward to help themselves. I used a few expletives while spouting off. Fr. Moody sat me down and set me straight. I had given them clothing which they had never used. I had imposed methods that they had never practiced. After I went back to America they would continue to carry on their customs. I was out of line trying to impress my standards on people who would never reach such standards in their everyday life.

I learned many lessons while away from home. Son Paul had hastily married and had a son whom he named Jonathon. My Mother was taken ill with lung cancer and died within four weeks of being diagnosed. People, dear to me, could be married, buried, and born without me. One believes they must do this or they must do that, but when time and distance come between what we must do and what we can do, every thing still gets accomplished. Life goes on with or without me.

Chapter 9
European Spree 1968

The contract with TEA ended in May of l968. The sea freight had to be packed and sent home. I intended to leave the household items like sheets, towels and the dishes with Bartholomew. That would leave room to pack interesting items such as the zebra drum coffee table (three feet in diameter) native carvings, hand-woven baskets as well as the dried seed pods I had been busily collecting. We contacted the German Lufthansa Air Travel Agency and planned an itinerary that included Italy, Austria, Switzerland, France and England.

We sold the cooker, the little refrigerator and other household items. Finally we sold the car. We banked the money from each transaction. A few days just before leaving, we learned that the government allowed just 200 shillings ($50) per person to leave the country. It would take a year for them to clear all accounts and make sure no debts were owed. How were we to manage to pay for our trip back home? All of our money was frozen. Fr. Moody came to our rescue. He suggested George write a check as a donation to the mission. George did and handed the check to Fr. Moody who returned the next day with English pounds, Canadian dollars and American dollars. Now we had the problem of how to carry so much cash. We solved that dilemma. Using the hem of a pillow case we made a money belt for George to wear around his waist under his shirt while we traveled. This arrangement would present a few problems along the way.

The day of departure arrived. The many friends we made came to the Mwanza Airport to see us off. Our plane was a propeller driven biplane that carried six passengers and was flown by a bush pilot from Texas. We flew over Lake Victoria with its many islands and floating papyrus beds to Entebbe, Uganda where we boarded a jet plane. We were to fly directly to Rome. Not so. The plane developed a minor problem, which was never explained to us, and had to land at Khartoum in the Sudan. Before landing everyone had to fill out a paper claiming the assets being carried. Even your wedding ring had to be declared! Oh, oh. What do we do? Claim the money or not. If we mention the money, could it be confiscated for illegally taking it out of Tanzania? We chanced it. We did not declare its presence. We were directed into the airport waiting room. It was late at night. It was hot and humid and oppressive. The dirty, dusty overhead fans were slowly circling trying to stir the air. Geoffrey was very thirsty. I attempted to get him an orange squash at the counter when George stopped us saying, "How dare you risk drinking anything that hasn't been boiled? We have boiled all of the water that we drank for two years and now you are going to let him drink this?" We walked away thirstier than ever.

A short time later we boarded the plane to continue on to Rome. We landed again, this time in Cairo, Egypt. Again we had to fill out the claim forms. Again we didn't mention the travel money. It is now sunrise. We could see the Great Pyramids from the plane. This was just another quick stop. We took off and this time landed in Athens, Greece. We got a view of the Acropolis as we landed. Our last stop was Rome. We arrived a full day late. We missed our scheduled visit to the Vatican! We were able to resume our planned itinerary and boarded a bus that would journey along the Amalfi Way. Beautiful scenery of tiny towns and huge cathedrals contrasted with the dry, barren land from which we had come.

George had spent a Rest and Recuperation assignment on the Island of Capri while he was serving in the European Theater of World War II. He had always promised me he would take me to see this glorious site one day. The day came. We visited the Blue Grotto. The weather was windy and grey, the water was choppy, but we made it into the watery luminous cave. It was a fantastic sight. George fulfilled his promise.

Returning to Capri, Patti and I noticed fabulous stores selling beautiful clothing and shoes. It had been two years since we had had any new clothing. We each found handsome knitted suits to purchase. George had to use the dressing room in the ladies' store to undress enough to get to the money belt with the funds pinned around his waist to pay the bill for those suits.

At the ruins of Pompeii I was struck with the contrast of a developed society that had plumbing three thousand years ago and yet today most of Africa is still without such an important necessity. The opulent public bath houses revealed a most sumptuous way of life ages and ages ago.

Our visit to Austria included a visit to a Cathedral, a castle, a rathskeller, vineyards, the Danube River, and a gondola ride up into the Alp Mountains with Strauss Waltzes filling the air. The beauty and cleanliness of their red tiled roofed housing was evident everywhere. It was truly a tourists' delight.

Next it was on to Switzerland, where we were scheduled for lunch atop Grindelwald First, one of the Swiss Alps. To get to the restaurant we had to take the ski lift. My acrophobia kicked in. I did not feel hungry. I suggested that I would wait in the tour bus while they enjoyed the excursion. Nothing doing. We were family and we had to stick together. Patti offered to take the responsibility of me. We were seated two together in the chair lift. George and Geoffrey climbed into the chair behind us. Off we went. It was a pleasant May day; the sun was shining and a cool breeze was blowing. The puffy white clouds decorated the clear blue sky. We passed over meadows where cows were grazing, we passed over brown chalets, we passed over tall evergreen trees until we came to an open shed. "That was not too bad a ride," I commented. But that wasn't the end. We had entered a relay station that sent us on our way up the mountain to the next station. There we were tossed heavy coats because the air was getting steadily colder. By the time we reached the third station, I begged the attendant to let me off. Not understanding that I was frightened, he tossed me another coat to keep warm. As we were leaving the fourth station we passed George and Geoffrey entering. I hollered, "I can't take this!" George replied, "Shut your eyes!" I did. We finally reached the top of the mountain and entered the restaurant.

The view from atop the world was purported to be fantastic. As we looked out, a blinding snow storm completely obstructed the view. By the time we finished lunch the storm had passed and the view was magnificent. Now we must descend. George rode with me down the mountain. He would describe the scenery that I was missing because my eyes were tight shut. Behind us in the next chair Patti and Geoffrey were swinging and singing, thoroughly enjoying the ride. When we reached the bottom and before returning to our seats on the bus my family performed a small private ceremony awarding me with a pin with a picture of the mountain for my 'bravery' beyond the call of duty.

Our travel to Paris had to be cancelled because of the workers riots of 1968. No Eiffel tower, no French maids. That gave us more time in London. We took it all in, from the changing of the Guard at Buckingham Palace to the dazzle of the crown jewels displayed in the Tower of London. We were there long enough to familiarize ourselves with the subway and bus system so we were able to get around as we chose. The time came to board the plane and jet back to America.

Chapter 10
Back to Endwell 1968

Our timetable centered on son Tom's graduation from Kings Point Maritime Academy. We just had to be in attendance for that occasion. We were. It was breath-taking to me to see the precision marching, the crisp white uniforms, the healthy, bright cadets under the American flag waving proudly in the open air. The contrast with our recent environment was startling. Everything worked, was on schedule and was sparkling clean! That was a proud moment in my life; proud of my country and proud of my son and his accomplishment.

We returned to Endwell and our house on Lorne Drive. The furniture was returned from storage. A few days of scrubbing and tending the yard, we were back to reality. Patti and Geoffrey returned to their schools. Patti was a senior in High School preparing to graduate within the month. New York State required the passing of State Regents Tests to qualify to graduate. Our school, Maine Endwell Central Schools, had sent materials to her to study while in Mwanza. Although she had spent a year and a half in the English boarding school and had successfully completed her lessons, even winning a scholastic prize presented by the President of Kenya, Jomo Kenyatta, she needed to conform to the program here. Patti fulfilled her requirements, graduated and was accepted into college.

I was anxious to meet our first grandchild, Jonathan. Paul, Jan and the baby had lived with Jan's parents ever since they had been married. Paul had changed colleges to be with his new family. The baby was three months old. I expected him to be rounded out, smiling and cooing. Instead he was a puny, pale sickly infant. I could tell right away he was not healthy. I took charge as soon as Paul and Jan left him with us while they looked for housing in Connecticut where Paul had just landed a job. I took Jonathan to the pediatrician who sent him to the hospital in Syracuse. He had a malfunction in his digestive system that took two weeks to correct. Paul and Jan took a healthy, happy baby to their new home.

Our oldest son Jim had spent so much of his time in Pensacola, Florida while in the Navy; the locals looked pretty good to him. He became engaged to Sharon while we were away. They delayed the wedding until his parents could attend. On a hot summer day in Pensacola they were married. As part of their honeymoon they spent some time with us in Endwell.

Another tragedy had occurred while we were out of the country. George's mother who had been living with her two sisters had suffered a stroke. When we were settled, we brought her to our home where we could take care of her. It was a massive stroke affecting her speech and movement of her right side. It was sad to see this once vibrant, peppy woman so limited. The loss of speech was extremely hard for her to endure. She was once again living in her old room with us. The tables had been turned. We were now taking care of her instead of her helping us.

One Saturday, George and I had business that took us out of the house. We explained to Granny Morris where we were going and promised to be back soon. She was sitting in a comfortable chair to watch television while we were gone. Geoffrey was at his friend's house. When we returned we found them sitting together. Geoffrey had his arm around her shoulders. He was eight years old but that didn't stop him from scolding us for leaving his grandmother alone. They truly loved each other.

George returned to his office and desk where he settled back into his job as Athletic Director. He had taken a leave of absence from Maine Endwell Schools to go to Africa. I had not considered a return to teaching because we had Granny to tend. However, I received a phone call from the principal of one of the district schools. He insisted I come to work for him taking a fourth grade assignment. I said I would need refresher courses in Modern Math. I had been engaged in Remedial Reading for so many years, I only knew about the new Math from others. He explained to me that his school was departmentalized. My curriculum area would be Language Arts for which I was well prepared and experienced. The salary offered was almost twice the salary I had earned just two years earlier. Knowing I could afford to hire help for Granny, I accepted the job.

Fall of 1968 found me back in the classroom, George in his former position, Patti enrolled in Community College and Geoffrey in third grade in the elementary school. All was well in Endwell.

George's mother began having mini-strokes. She was hospitalized three times. The last time she passed away. Her two sisters, Mildred and Lila came by plane from Swarthmore, Pennsylvania to say their final goodbyes. Both in their late sixties, they were dressed to the nines in fur coats, spike heels and upswept hair-dos. Oh how they cried and even wailed at the funeral service. Later, at dinner, at our house, they spoke about what a good job they did mourning their sister. They made the comment that they should hire out for funerals. They were that good at mourning. Those three sisters were a comedy act in themselves. It was fun to be around them even on a sad occasion.

As the 1969 school year began winding to an end, we talked about taking a vacation to see our own country's sights. We had a month's time for travel. It would be too costly to stay in motels or hotels and buy every meal at a restaurant for that length of time. Someone suggested we could rent a travel trailer. The overnight campsite rent was far less than a motel for the four of us. Tom was able to go along with George, Geoffrey and me. We could also prepare our own meals. We spent some time looking into that way to travel and found that renting a trailer and insurance was costly, too. After much discussion we decided to buy a simple pop-up trailer. We could sell it after the trip if we found we didn't enjoy traveling that way. Like it? We spent the next fourteen years trailering. Every few years we traded up until we reached the level of Airstream, the epitome of travel comfort at that time.

A whole new world opened up for us. Before we could begin traveling, we had to learn how to operate this camper. We took weekend trips to campsites in the nearby Catskill Mountains. We had had a trailer hitch and electrical equipment installed on the car. When we took the first left hand turn to go down the hill of Pheasant Lane and stopped for the intersection with Hooper Road, we heard and felt a thud. Checking out the problem, it was discovered the trailer wasn't correctly hitched to the car causing it to ram the license plate on the car. Nothing major. The adjustment was made and we continued. The trailer pulled smoothly with no further problems until we reached the campsite. George had no idea how to back up into the camping space. After a few bad attempts and assistance from the campsite manager, he soon learned the knack of backing up with an attachment to the car. We had a very pleasant weekend. There was a gas range to cook our food, the electricity lighted up the room well enough to read, the built in gas heater warmed us and the water flowed from the hook-up. This was as good as home, almost. George did some fly-fishing for trout, we hiked along the trails, we played board games and had a good night's sleep. We liked it! From then on any free weekend found us on the road. We were ready for cross-country traveling.

Our destination of the summer in 1969 was Yellowstone

National Park. The first night found us in Ohio. We stopped around four o'clock in order to set up before dark. George, Tom, the recent graduate engineer, and Geoffrey began opening the camper for the night. The bed boards had to be pulled out, one on each end of the boxlike body of the trailer, the canvas stretched overhead after the roof had been hand cranked to its fullest height. The lifelines were attached; water and electric, and Geoffrey hung the step. The whole process was completed in less than five minutes. Mom could now cook dinner. It was so nice; we were together in our home away from home. The next morning as I prepared breakfast the "men" began to close up the camper. They were finished almost before the washed dishes were put away. In fact, they were sitting in the car ready to go and I didn't get a chance to brush my teeth. From then on I called an end to this race against the clock while closing or opening the camper.

It was a delightful trip. Staying right in the wilderness in the beautiful scenery was wonderful. One felt like a part of the surroundings instead of just a sightseer. Geoffrey really got "hooked" on trout fishing at Slough Creek. George had no time to fish himself; he was too busy removing the fish from Geoff's hook. He was catching a fish as soon as his line hit the water. In spite of the good fishing, we had to leave. The mosquitoes were biting as fast, or faster than the fish, harder too.

Watching Old Faithful erupt on schedule shooting white, steaming rivers of water high into the air was phenomenal. It is remarkable to think of its regularity year after year, long before man had discovered it. The other thermal pools sputtering and steaming and erupting kept us entertained as well. Old Spiteful, a very small bubbling spring, caught me off guard and spit right into my face as I was looking down into it. The family had a good laugh over that.

Visiting Yellowstone National Park was the goal of our

summer vacation, but we enjoyed so much more: The Badlands, Mt. Rushmore, Rocky Mt. National Park and Dinosaur Park. Each stay provided us sights and pleasures we had only heard about and now experienced ourselves. The whole trip did not break the bank. Overnight stops were very reasonable especially an overnight stay in a Wisconsin City Park was just a dollar and a half per night. Arriving safely home, we definitely wanted to keep the camper. We found a campground about an hour's drive away in the Catskill Mts. Where we parked the camper the "men" could enjoy more fishing. It would be their choice where to go: the East branch of the Delaware River, the Pepacton Reservoir, the Beaverkill River or the Willowemoc River. Many, many weekends were spent at Terry's Campground at Shinhopple, New York.

The 1969-70 school year began in September. Our family was gradually spreading out. Jim was stationed in Pensacola, Florida and had set-up housekeeping with his new bride, Sharon. Tom was sailing around the world as an engineer on transport ships. Paul, Jan and Jonathon were living in New Britain, Connecticut where he was employed by Pratt and Whitney. Patti was attending her last year of Junior College. George, Geoff and I were back in the Maine Endwell School District. Everyone was busy. The year passed quickly.

Patti and Gary Schanz met that year and became best friends and lovers. They completed their educations at different colleges, she at SUNY Cortland and he at SUNY Binghamton. They became engaged to marry at Christmas time. Gary went on to Graduate School of Law at Syracuse and Patti began her teaching career at Moravia. His mother died suddenly. It was a blow to Gary. He almost quit Law School. He wanted to get married immediately. He was not sure what to do. There was so much self-doubt, confusion and pressure they decided to part. It was more than either one of them could handle. Gary returned to his studies. Patti went to Europe to study for the summer.

121

Another trip to fish the western streams was made by just George, Geoffrey and me. The year was 1972. Geoff, now a capable 12 year old young man, filled the role of navigator. I was relegated to the back seat of the car as he occupied the seat next to the driver. He did an excellent job until we hit the Big Horn Mountain Range. He chose an alternate route which was more direct to our destination. We began a climb reminiscent of the Amalfi Drive in Italy. That was in a tour bus that had to back-up in order to make the switchback turns up the mountain. We were pulling a travel trailer hauling it around the switchbacks on gravel roads. The deep snow in the mountain pass had just been plowed out and the pass opened for the summer. George held his breath while we started the decent down the other side. He had to negotiate sharp switchbacks, steep declines and sheer precipices. He never dared take his eyes off the road to take in the magnificent scenery.

This trip was planned around the information found in McClean's Encyclopedia of Fishing, a gift I had given George. The waters they cast into were the Madison (where Geoff was frightened by antelope), the Yellowstone, the Shoshone, the Snake and the Gros Ventre. Geoffrey was amazed at the specific directions given in the Encyclopedia. The paths, the rocks, the trees, and the pools of water were exactly as described in the book. I enjoyed watching the two of them cast flies, swinging out all that line and resting it quietly on the surface of the water. They caught many rainbow and cutthroat trout. The fishing was so good we had enough to share dinner with two bicyclists who were camped near us.

We spent some time in Jackson Hole, Wyoming. It was rustic at the time. Tackle and bait shops, guides and fishing trips were the main commerce. Souvenir hunting offered elk horns and jack-o-lopes. Geoffrey really was taken in by that offer. He wanted to see the real animal instead of a mounted specimen. He didn't appreciate the old timers poking fun of him believing there was such a species when there never was such an animal. The taxidermists had attached small horns to the jack rabbit head and called it a jack-a-lope.

Our journey ended on the North Rim of the Grand Canyon. We set up our trailer home in the Kaibab Forest. It was abundant with black squirrels with white tails, pine trees and aspens. Our highlight was a mule ride down Bright Angel Trail. I loved using the story "Brighty of the Grand Canyon" in my reading classes. Riding on the back of a sure-footed jack or jenny, peering over the head, looking between the upright ears into open canyons was exciting and frightening. The paths were very narrow and crumbling. Crews were working constantly to rebuild them. It was just a wonderland of colored walls, shapes and crevices unbelievably carved by wind and water.

Our last stop was at Carlsbad Caverns, where every evening millions of bats fly out of the mouth of the cave to feed all night. Eerie and frightening, they made a faint whirring sound as they escaped the cave at a rate of thousands per minute.

Bryce Canyon National Park 1973

Our journey over, we returned home by way of Interstate 10, the southern highway through New Mexico, Texas, Alabama and Florida where we visited son Jim and his wife in Pensacola. Summer was over. School began again for all of us. Every school year was the same, but also different. My focus was the classroom and George was concerned with the sports programs. He had coached the basketball teams during the winter and track teams during the spring. As Athletic Director, he supervised, staffed and scheduled all sports activities. School and athletics filled our lives. The children had set out on their own life-courses, leaving us behind.

Patti and Gary had begun dating again and were again engaged to marry. The big day was set for August 24, 1974. Patti had been teaching in Moravia while Gary completed his law degree. Neither of them had a job. They had applications in, but no commitments. The day before the wedding that problem was solved. Patti was hired to teach Physical Education in the Susquehanna School District and

Gary was appointed clerk to the judge.

As the bells rang out from the steeple of Endwell Methodist Church, George handed over his precious daughter in marriage to Gary Schanz. It was a beautiful candle-lit ceremony. The bride was pretty and petite, a living doll. The ceremony and reception went on without a hitch. They were off on their honeymoon to Okracoke, on the Outer Banks of North Carolina. Her father had been most generous, writing checks for all the expenditures without question. He outdid himself. A true father-of-the-bride.

Since his graduation from the Kings Point Academy in 1968, Tom had been working as an engineer on transport ships that took him around the world more than once. He would leave the ship when in port for unloading and reloading and make jaunts into the different countries and cultures. He brought presents to us at home, opals for his sister, stamps and a telescope for his little brother and a set of Norataki china for his mother. Since the ships did not stop working for the weekend, two days per week were added to his vacation time. Once on leave, he would be home as long as three months at a time. He put that time to good use by doing home improvements on our house. He built a spacious family room in the basement. Another vacation he remodeled a downstairs bedroom into a den by removing the double closet and building in a desk and bookcases. One vacation he had so much time he accepted a part-time job at a company that designed exhaust systems for nuclear waste.

This neat arrangement soon ended. The shipping company revamped their ships into container ships which cut down on the unloading and loading time in port. His last sail was in the North Atlantic. He was aboard for almost a full year without his feet ever touching land. He decided to give up sailing. He returned to college for another degree in Construction Management. While there he found himself a girl to marry.

Morris children 1976   Jim, Tom, Paul, Geoff, and Patti

On January 3, 1976 Tom married Sharon Nichols. It was the stormiest day of the year. The church steps were deeply covered with snow. There were numerous traffic accidents involving more than one vehicle. We, the family, all made it for the lovely wedding and reception. It was such a happy time. We didn't realize the weather would be symbolic of their marriage. It was a stormy one.

Chapter 11
Retirement 1977

George celebrated his 57th birthday. Thoughts of retirement began to swirl in his head. He did not want to repeat his father's mistake of waiting too long until forced to leave because of ill health. George wanted to enjoy a few years of recreation while he was still healthy and hearty. At this time a new Superintendent of Schools was hired who really annoyed and discouraged George. He was a very negative person. He took over the right to a vote in STAC, the regional sports association which George had helped organize thirty years previously. It was an embarrassment to George to loose that privilege. George had reached his peak of professional status as Athletic Director, he had no further ambitions. Mulling over all of these considerations in his head, he began to think more and more about retirement. The big day came in June. He loved his freedom from hassles, from putting in long days on the job and from making decisions that affected so many.

I was still too young to retire with benefits, but that didn't bother him. He accepted retirement. He really enjoyed taking Geoff fishing and hunting whenever he chose. When inclement weather interfered, he enjoyed reading or puttering around the house. One day he decided to surprise me by doing the laundry. That should have pleased me to have him helping. He did three loads of laundry and there they sat piled in baskets, over-dried and wrinkled. Most of the items had to be rewashed to remove the deep, dried wrinkles. I then asked him to stick to his gun cleaning and fly-tying. It created more work to salvage things from his efforts. He had the nerve to say, "What's so hard about laundry? You just put clothes in the washer and move them to the dryer!"

George would really be happier when I could also retire so

we could do things together, like travel. I was now turning 55 and I had twenty five years of teaching behind me. I was eligible to retire. What about our son Geoffrey? He had one more year of high school. We can't abandon him, can we? What if he was in an accident? What if he began using drugs? What if his marks lowered? How could I leave my baby? Yet, I did!!

As it happened, that year there were budget problems in the schools. Class size was increased and teachers were being let go. To avoid firings, all of the teachers who qualified were urged to retire. There I was, in the middle as usual. I loved my teaching job. I was good at it, too. The pressures of the administration, of George and even Geoffrey convinced me my time had come. Geoffrey claimed he didn't want the guilt trip if we were never able to retire because of him. I became a retiree in 1977.

Although it may have seemed like a rash move, we had spent a few years making plans as to what, where and how we would live the rest of our lives. The first requirement was to have the house in tip top shape. While we were still at maximum salary, we had a new roof put on the house, a fresh coat of paint and new rugs laid throughout the living room, entrance and hallways. We also bought our retirement vehicle: the Airstream Argosy. It was well equipped and streamlined in design for easier towing. We also purchased a new big car to pull it, a Buick Electra 455.

What about Geoffrey? I had suggested earlier that he graduate from High School now, he had more than enough credits and was taking Advanced Placement courses. He didn't like that idea. He wanted to graduate with his class. He offered to stay in the house on his own or go stay with his sister and her husband in the next town. That was out because he couldn't go to his same school while living out of the district. The final solution was for Patti and Gary to come live with him in our house. Gary insisted this was not just a month's vacation we were taking because he had to end his lease for the townhouse they were renting. We then agreed to stay away a year.

George had a great time plotting our vagabond year. The fishing encyclopedia was open; road maps and the atlas were spread out. I was sure that I would never see the bright lights of a city again. We'd be forever parked beside a stream somewhere.

Geoffrey spent the summer traveling with us as he always had. He put the pressure on me to quit smoking. He threatened to stay home so he wouldn't be exposed to second hand smoke in the car and trailer. I had to stop that nasty habit. George had quit as soon as he retired. I was the culprit now. I tried very hard, slipping back now and again, but I was smoke free when the school year was over.

Leaving on retirement trip, June 1977

By the end of June 1977, the retirement party was over, my desk was cleaned out, twenty five years of teaching mementos were packed away, good-byes were said and the key was turned in the lock of the trailer. We were on our way searching for fun and adventure. The second day found us driving in a violent hail and thunderstorm on the outskirts of Chicago. It was so dark and raining so hard the visibility was nil. Slowly, we persevered until the storm ended. When we stopped for fuel, George noticed the paint on the crown of the trailer was missing in many areas, just peeled away. That was a violent storm! I know I hardly took a breath while its violence continued, fearing an accident.

We continued our travels. Our meanderings took us to places we had been before and to places we had never visited. Beautiful scenery of mountains, rivers, rock formations and the erosion from wind and water filled our days. Of course, each destination was well-known for its fishing.

Thursday was the day we would call home to check on things. Patti and Gary were ensconced in the house taking care of the mail, paying the bills and maintaining the house and lawns. About the fifth week out Patti told Geoff that his friends had come by hoping he had returned. That planted the idea in his head and heart that he was homesick and was ready to return. We drove to the airport at Missoula, Montana and made arrangements for his flight home. That was too much for me to handle. I broke down and cried and cried. I scared myself because I couldn't stop. Somehow it seemed to be the end of my life: no house to keep, no school to go to, and now no family to tend. It felt like a death had occurred. I was having a rough time.

We drove on to Rock Creek, Montana, where we would spend the night. I was still sobbing. Reality had set in, my life was over. Everything that was me was gone. After an early

130

supper, the men went to the stream to fish. Still crying, I went to the camp store and bought a package of cigarettes. I found a solitary spot in the woods and smoked one cigarette after another until I stopped the crying.

The next day we put Geoff on the plane for home. George devoted the next two months to me. It was wonderful, the honeymoon trip we never had. We traveled on to Glacier National Park where we stayed a few days taking in the remarkable beauty on our daily hikes together. Then continuing on through the Canadian Parks of Yoho and Jasper we saw bear, moose, elk and mountain goats. While still in Jasper, we rode the snowcat out onto Athabasca Glacier. I shall never forget peering deep down into the fissure, a sparkling blue, blue river of ice. It was a feeling of being in the Ice Age. My imagination could visualize the animals trapped in these miles and miles of ice that seemed to extend to the center of the earth. It was a most moving experience.

We continued our drive westward passing through Alberta Province leisurely camping at parks and private campgrounds. George suggested we better get moving along. I could not understand why when we were retired and had no place to be. He merely said, "We have mountains to cross and we don't want to get caught in the snow." It was the middle of September. Not dallying to see this or that, we crossed British Columbia and made it to Vancouver. While there in a big metropolis we located an Air Stream Center. We were having some trouble with the water pump, so this made a good place to have it repaired.

Westport, Washington was where we next set up for a night or two. I was now quite recovered from my separation anxieties, so George sought a salmon fishing day trip to book. I was not interested in accompanying him, I am not a good seaman. I drove him to the dock with rain pelting the windshield. The weatherman on the radio said it was misting. When I picked George up at the docks in late afternoon he proudly exhibited his salmon catch, too many pounds to eat fresh. There were men roaming the area trying to buy the salmon roe that they peddled as caviar. In order to preserve the fish, George had the fish smoked and canned.

Moving on we settled in a site east of Seattle. It was necessary to replete our finances. We opened an account in the bank with a generous check from our home account. When the check cleared which took about four or five days, we would draw out the funds and close the account and move on. ATM's did not exist in 1977. While we waited for funds, we visited sights in and around Seattle going to the Space Needle and Mount Rainier National Park. The weather had cleared giving us some sun-filled September days. Near our location blackberries were growing wild. The canes were over eight feet tall and drooped from the weight of the biggest, most luscious blackberries I have ever tasted.

Back on the road, George stopped at a fishing sport shop in Oregon. Orvis offered fishing equipment that one could tryout on the man-made pond. He enjoyed himself and bought some more fly tying materials and other "toys". The word in the store was the steelheads were running up the Santiam River at Sweet Home. All excited with anticipation of some great sport, George located a camp site not far from the river. The word was gospel to George. You could have walked on the backs of the fish to cross the water. The fish were thick. It was a sight to watch the silvery rainbow trout returning from the sea swim up over that dike to spawn in fresh water. It was my fisherman's paradise!

George caught a 32 inch steelhead weighing 9 lbs. He used a green-butted skunk fly lure purchased at Orvis. He had several other good catches including a Chinook salmon. What shall we do with all this fish? The fishing encyclopedia contained a whole chapter on preserving your catch. We purchased a small electric smoker, apple chips, salt, brown sugar, and spices, as well as a dozen pint canning jars. For two weeks he fished every day and I preserved the bounty.

Back on the road, we progressed along Highway 1 through the twists and turns following the Pacific coastline. Every turn revealed another picturesque view. We set up at a state campsite right on the bluff overlooking the Pacific Ocean. It was noisy with the sound of giant waves smashing against huge rocks. Walking along the narrow beach down at ocean side and clambering over the great rock formations, it was fabulous to observe nature. There on the leeside of the giant rocks in the quiet little pools were hermit crabs skittering around ignoring the powerful movement elsewhere on the same rocks. Life exists wherever it can.

We spent more than a month in Oregon. We dug clams at Bandon when the neap tide revealed more of the beach that is usually covered by the ocean. One had to buy a license .Equipment needed were rented out, namely a spade, a pail and a measure. I thought George would reach China with his spade at the pace he set. The beach was crowded with clam diggers. The strategy was to site a small air hole in the sand, which indicated the location of a clam, marking where one should dig. A clam was usually found, but it had to be large enough to be legal to keep. If not, it had to be reburied in order to grow bigger. Several environmental and game wardens paroled the beach to make sure the rules were obeyed.

Another day was spent down at a dock crabbing. Again rental equipment was available. A baited line was dropped at the end of the dock and when you felt movement you carefully, slowly, drew in the line. If you pulled too fast the crab would drop off. Smoothly a net was placed in the water under the crab so when it dropped off it would land in the net. We also baited a crab trap. When we drew that out of the water we dumped it onto the dock. Quickly, we examined each one to identify its sex before they scooted off the dock and back into the water. Only males were keepers.

All of these delicacies were thoroughly enjoyed when prepared back in the travel trailer. Oregon also grew monster oysters. We did not gather those ourselves. We purchased them at the packing house. We enjoyed gourmet delights of oyster Rockefeller, oyster Benedict and oyster stew, as well as crab cakes and chowder.

Returning to Highway 1, we made our way into California and the famed Redwood forests. Typical tourists now, we took the drive through a huge redwood tree, visited the house and souvenir shop in the base of a huge tree and looked up and up and up to the tops of these giant trees. We spent the night at Salt Point State Park. There we encountered scuba divers in wetsuits armed with spears riding on sea kayaks. They were catching the albacore that abide in the coastal areas of the ocean. We also heard the barking of sea lions. One such animal was sunning himself on the sun-bleached sandy beach. When we resumed our drive southward we came to a refuge for sea lions. We stopped in for a look. Hundreds of sea lions flopped on the beach and swam in the water. Every adult and pup was barking in full voice echoing through the whole building. It was so loud we didn't linger very long.

By October, we arrived in Marin County, California. We located a travel trailer park; registered and set up for the week we expected to stay. The water supply had been in the tank since September when we began our west coast journey. George thought it was a good time to empty the tank and disinfect it before refilling. We had no need to use that water supply because a fresh water hook-up was available at each site. He removed the plug and let the water drain. What a hullabaloo befell as the owner of the park and the office staff came running at us. We had no clue that Marin County was under strict orders to conserve water as they were experiencing a severe drought. The stream of water coming from our trailer and running across the parking lot was as valuable as gold in the rain-starved area. George closed the drain, but the finger of water kept pointing to the culprit trailer all morning. If authorities had seen it, the trailer park owner would have had to pay a stiff fine. The water shortage was so bad, we later learned, the City Hall erected a building-sized chart to record the progress in conserving water. Their motto was: If it's yellow, let it mellow; if it's brown, flush it down.

In spite of our embarrassing entrance, we thoroughly enjoyed the Bay Area. I had my hair shaped and permed. We celebrated our 35th wedding anniversary at a fine restaurant overlooking the bay. We took the cable car ride but could not go to Chinatown. It was cordoned off because of what was called a Tong War. Separate gangs of Chinese were having territorial turf fighting. There was plenty more to see and do in this fine city on the bay. We went wine tasting in Sonoma Valley, wandered through Fisherman's Wharf and took the boat tour around the bay.

Continuing our California journey, we visited Disneyland in Anaheim. The sun was very late in poking through, eleven o'clock! It dawned on us that it took that long to burn through the smog. While riding in the sight-seeing Disney car the driver told us that Bing Crosby had just died. That brought back memories of my dad and his dislike of Bing's singing. Dad had called it groaning and moaning. He liked the full exuberant voice of Nelson Eddy. We kids loved Bing, his singing and his songs.

The time had come to find a place to spend the winter. It was getting late in October. Storms would likely be due at this time of year inhibiting travel. We decided to cross over the San Bernardino Mountains to the desert area and look for a resting place for the winter. We arrived in the city of Palm Springs. We referred to our guide to trailer parks and following directions came to a cozy-looking settlement. It was the Golden Sands Mobile Home Park with an area near the swimming pool set aside for travel trailers. When I went into the office to register I was asked how long we wished to stay. I replied, "We'll try it for a week and if we like it we will stay the winter."

"Oh, no you won't", I was told. "We are booked solid for the winter, beginning right after the holidays. You may stay until then if you wish."

We chose a site and George began maneuvering to back the trailer into the parking area. Being experienced trailer-people, we no longer shouted directions. We now used hand signals to indicate the corrections needed to manipulate into position. Nothing draws a crowd of onlookers faster than yelling to one another. As quiet and organized as we were, there was still a small gathering in the pool area watching our movements. We no sooner hooked up the lifelines of water, sewer and electricity when they called out, "Hurry get your suits on and get over here in the pool!" That was the enthusiasm we enjoyed while we stayed there. They were a great bunch of retirees living it up.

An easy-going schedule soon developed. Be at the pool by ten. Lunch was around noon. Afterward, take a siesta for an hour or so. Then back to the pool by two. Drinks and hors d'oeuvres appeared around four. Dinner plans were discussed and made. It was a lazy life. We enjoyed lots of sun, lots of food, lots of reading and lots of laughter. Soon George and I discovered our waistlines were expanding. We then incorporated an early morning walk around the golf course that surrounded the trailer park. We did not play golf, but enjoyed the walk bright and early each morning.

Each weekend we took ourselves on short visits to nearby areas. We drove to Andreas Canyon, an oasis with huge palm trees, towering high over the dry barren desert with shaggy trunks as big as barns. There we ate our picnic lunch

136

amid swarms of hummingbirds of every size and color. Another Sunday we were driving the Palms-to-Pines Highway climbing higher and higher when we came upon a group of hang gliders. They were gathered atop a canyon edge with their colorful gliders awaiting the thermals that would allow them to soar out over the desert and return. We watched rather than accept an offer of a ride.

We learned the sex life of the date palm when we stopped at a date farm. It is quite an undertaking to bag up the newly ripened blossoms to keep the trees from cross-breeding. Most of the pollination is done by hand. It was there I tasted the most wonderful date, a luscious Majool. Other excursions found us at a grapefruit ranch in Pushwalla.

Time passed quickly. The Christmas season was looming. How would I ever cope with being so distant from family and home? George solved that by having Geoffrey fly out to be with us. That was a very thoughtful gift from him to me. I decorated the travel trailer with a Nativity scene that Patti had made from felt by hand and sent to me. I created a cornhusk wreath which hung in the big window with a few colored lights. It was very festive.

It was another hot and dry Christmas reminiscent of Christmas in Tanzania. No snow, no white Christmas. Yet, we solved that problem by taking the tramway up the San Jacinto Mountains to the icy and snowy fields overlooking the desert below. It was a fabulous Christmas dining with Geoff and George at a fine restaurant high up in the clouds. Too soon Geoffrey had to return to school and we had to move on.

We had found a camp site available in Mesa, Arizona. The payment of a month's rent in advance held it open until our arrival. New Year's Eve found us enjoying a dance in one of the clubhouses. This trailer park was enormous. So big it needed two large clubhouses, two swimming pools, and two

137

hot tubs. It accommodated one thousand travel trailers. Each parking space was provided a cement patio, a young palm tree and a mailbox on a post next to the road. This was big business. It was named Trailer Village II. There was a Trailer Village I about a mile away. Built on old fruit ranches, the villages housed snowbirds from many cold climates. They came from the United States, Canada and abroad. Many amenities were offered; including woodworking shops, lapidaries, square dancing lessons, tap dancing lessons, exercise classes and water aerobics. With so much to do the rest of the winter went quickly.

Exercise group in parade 1978

George and I continued our Sunday drives. We visited Superstition Mountain, Apache Trail, an old gold mine, The San Xavier Mission and made a trip into Mexico. We enjoyed Scottsdale, its gardens and the Parada Del Sol parade and rodeo. One could not escape the desert. Everywhere you went was desert. My first impression was that it was depressing. It was hot sun, dry sand, strong winds and barren. It began to mellow on me the more time we spent in it. By the time spring arrived, I had fallen in love with it. It bloomed and bloomed and bloomed. What had appeared dead and dried up now exploded into a myriad of color. Drifts of red poppies were everywhere. Each cactus showed off beautiful blooms. I needed a guide to identify the varied plants to learn their names and their habitats. I became acquainted with the red blossoms of the Firebush, the clumps of white Desert Daisies, the yellow poppies, the rose-colored Hedgehog blooms, the pink flowers of the Beavertail, the yellow adornment setting atop the Barrel cactus. All this and the interesting shapes and forms of the Chain Fruit Cholla, the Ocotillo and the majestic, pipe organ look of the Saguaro surrounded by golden marigolds, deep purple lupines and orange-tinged wild hollyhock. It had become the Bloomin' Desert.

Now that spring had arrived, we had to think about getting back home. We had gathered our life-lines and gear neatly into travel mode and drove away from our winter headquarters. It was after lunch time when we started out. Leaving the busy world of retirement we moseyed on our way toward New York. Fifty miles down the road we pulled into a primitive camp site at Picacho Peak State Park. We learned from reading the state marker that this was the site of a Civil War encounter. The only inhabitants of the area now were wild donkeys. Whether they were remnants of army mules or prospectors' animals we did not know. We soon learned they were beggars. Obviously other travelers had fed them so they expected the same from us. A bit of bread tossed far away got them away from our doorway so we could enter.

Bright and early at sunrise, we were once again heading out. We followed Interstate 10 for days through New Mexico and endless Texas. We did not take any side trips for sight-seeing. However, we did stop and stay a few days when we hit Pensacola, Florida. Our oldest son, Jim was still living there with his wife, Sharon. Jim was in the Navy assigned to Pensacola Naval Air station. He and wife Sharon had two sons, David and Eric. We needed to get to know them better. They lived so far away we only saw them a few days a year. We stayed four or five days getting reacquainted. Then we headed toward Birmingham and Knoxville where we picked up Interstate 81 heading north to Binghamton.

It was wonderful to see the hills of home again. Soon, we had a wedding to attend in Connecticut. Paul and Gayle were married on May 6th 1977.

Patti and Gary had done a wonderful job of parenting Geoffrey. He had matured into an out-going confident young man. He had not neglected his studies while socializing. He became the Valedictorian of his graduating class. It was not clear who was the proudest of having raised him so well, Patti or me. She had so enjoyed taking care and guiding him through the difficult year of possible senioritis, she intended to continue in that role. We all proudly attended his graduation ceremony.

There were other adjustments to make. Two families were staying in the same house. George had parked the travel trailer back at Terry's in the Catskill Mountains. We spent most of our time there to stay out of Patti and Gary's way. We still had to face the reality of where Pat and Gary would next live. They had saved a small nest egg for a down payment on a house of their own, but in 1978 there were high interest rates with inflation that tightened mortgage down payments. They did not have enough saved for the house they wanted. Another consideration, Patti was pregnant. There was no way we would make them move out. George and I were already talking of spending the next winter in Florida in our trailer, so they might just as well stay in the house.

Summer went quickly. We took a jaunt through the Adirondack Mountains with the travel trailer fishing the Ausable River, staying at Wilmington Notch, and looking at the preparations for the coming 1980 Winter Olympics at Lake Placid. Geoffrey was right there with his Dad whipping the fly line over the stream. Then the time came to move our last child into his dorm at college. Our task of child-raising was finally over. Thirty four years of happy, worrisome, joyful, and fulfilling child rearing had come to an end for us as he entered Cornell University.

October 26, 1978 Matthew was born to Patti and Gary. He was our fourth grandchild. He was the first to be near to us. In fact, we were all living in the same house. He was a perfectly beautiful baby with silky, blonde hair, bright blue eyes and a full round face. George and I took our turns walking the floor with him when he was colicky. It was he who gave me the nickname I have had ever since. When we returned from the South the next year he would hear me come into the house. To get me to come to him he would just shout, "GEEE-GEEE". It is Gigi that I have been called ever since.

As winter approached we hooked the travel trailer to the car and took off for warmer climes. We had been studying trailer magazines and travel brochures. We chose Homestead, the last town on the Florida peninsula before the Keys. We had selected and made reservations at the Goldcoaster Trailer Park. It was a long three-day drive for George. There was no way I would drive the car with that big rig trailing behind. We found the Goldcoaster Park ideal for the winter months. All the amenities were there; a large clubhouse, swimming pool, hot tub, large lots, gorgeous weather, and, as always, friendly travelers. It wasn't long before we were participating in a square dance class. George had found new fishing buddies. I busied myself with craft workshops and card playing. We continued our practice of weekend jaunts exploring the area. We were delighted to be so near the

Everglades National Park. Many hours were spent there with the exotic wildlife and tropical vegetation.

We certainly didn't travel light. George needed several fishing rods and reels, as well as a full tackle box. I needed my sewing machine, knitting needles and the tools and materials for craft projects. Our bicycles were carried on the back of the trailer and the 12 foot aluminum boat traveled on the top of the car. We were ready for whatever opportunities might arise. We always used everything we brought along.

We spent many hours putt-putting with a small outboard motor on West Lake in the Everglades fishing for whatever would bite; bass, brie, trout, sheep's head, or parrot fish. What made it more exciting were the alligators keeping a watch on us as we kept an eye on them. Many days we drove all the way to Flamingo on Florida Bay to try our luck catching blue crabs. There always seemed to be something to do, see and enjoy. It was a great life!

However, when spring came we were anxious to return north to be with family. Again we set up at Terry's Camp. George began fishing his favorite streams and the reservoir. I busied myself picking wild berries to make jams and jellies. The strawberries ripened first, followed by red raspberries, blueberries, black caps, and blackberries. I prepared enough jars to give Christmas presents to my new friends in Florida and still had plenty for us.

On the Fourth of July every one of our children and grandchildren joined us camping. We had a Morris Compound of tents and tent-trailers around our trailer. It was so great to be together. The children had now spread out: Jim and family were still in Pensacola, Tom and Sharon were in Syracuse, Paul and Gayle were in Connecticut, Patti and Gary were still in Endwell, and Geoffrey, home from college, stayed with us. Our group now numbered fifteen. For several years after that first campout, we continued to get together, until we became greater in number and more scattered.

By the time we were ready to return to the Goldcoaster in Florida, we were grandparents two more times. Jennifer was born to Gayle and Paul that summer and Jessica to Sharon and Tom later in the fall. We welcomed them into the world and our family before we traveled south.

We pulled into the rest stop and welcome center in North Carolina for a break. While there, we were drawn to the posters and pamphlets about the Outer Banks. Commenting that we had never been there, we decided to spend a few days exploring. A few hours later we pulled into a campground at Manteo. After getting set up and hooked up, we strolled around the grounds. We came across two couples fishing for perch in a little pond. We all introduced ourselves; the Browns from Ohio and the Fischers from New Jersey. The men were planning to dig oysters the next day while the women attended a Christmas craft session. George and I were invited to tag along. So started friendships that lasted until death parted us. We spent the next two weeks right there sight-seeing, dining, and chatting. The beauty of trailering is the flexibility one has to either go or stay as desired.

At the end of the third year at the Goldcoaster, the park was gradually changing from a travel trailer park to a manufactured home development. There was also the problem of expensive gasoline. A severe shortage had caused lines of cars to wait their turn at any station that was lucky enough to have fuel. Word would get out that a certain place had gas and the cars would be there like bees to honey. The Buick's large engine burned a gallon of gas every nine miles while drawing the trailer. George began to think seriously about purchasing a home at the Goldcoaster. I protested at first, and then agreed. When we were back with Patti and Gary that summer, we sold them our house and

143

ordered the model of home we had decided upon.

House at the Goldcoaster, Homestead, Fla 1984

This purchase made us true snowbirds. We winterized the trailer by draining all the pipes and filling them with antifreeze. We left it parked at Terry's Campsite for the winter and just drove to Florida in our car. We were delighted to see the home set up on our lot when we arrived. When the moving van delivered our furniture, a few weeks of cleaning and settling in and we were set for the season. Now with more rooms and two bathrooms, the visitors came. Each one of our children and their families visited us for at least one week. Friends also came and stayed a few days. It was great. We danced, fished and entertained in the glorious sunshine while winter held its wintry blast up north.

December, 1982 another grandson was born. He was named Andrew by his parents Tom and Sharon. Paul and Gayle had had another daughter, Rachel, in 1981. Pat and Gary completed their family with Stephen and Michael. That ended the new babies for a while. Our family had grown to number nineteen! Now we began the down cycle. Tom and Sharon parted as had Paul and his first wife, Jan. This was very difficult for me to handle. George suggested we go off by ourselves again to the great open spaces of the West.

Rather than uproot the big trailer that had settled into a corner under the trees with a big deck, awning and even a small garden, we borrowed Tom's pop-up trailer for the trip. We again saw Old Faithful spew her steam. We visited my sister Edith and her husband Arthur who had retired to Wyoming. The fishing was difficult; most of the popular spots had been posted by private owners with No Trespassing signs. On our way home we spent the hottest night of our entire lives in Goodman, Kansas. We pulled out of there before the sun came up and headed for home. George began to plan our next western tour. We would fly out to a private fishing camp with plenty of good fishing on their posted stream. He remarked, "There will be activities provided for you, I'm sure."

On our return to Florida, George had an appointment with Dr. Pena to check his blood pressure. He was on medication to keep it under control. While in the office George turned to me and said, "Now tell the Doctor about your problem." I had been experiencing some pressure from unreleased gas. I just figured I was tense from the family problems. That excuse wouldn't do. I was sent to the hospital for tests. Sure enough, a suspicious growth was discovered and I was admitted.

Three days of this test or that test each needing an enema before proceeding, I would ask each nurse as she appeared in my room, "Are you friend or enema?" It was determined that I had colon cancer. The night before the surgery Dr. Pena visited me. He assured me that he would be present in the operating room and with God's help all would be fine. "I'm afraid God won't give me any attention because I have ignored him for several years." I declared. Dr. Pena sat on my bed and repeated the story of the prodigal son. He expressed the deep depth of degradation the son had endured being a Jew who had to live with the pigs! Yet his father welcomed him back. Dr. Pena assured me I would be welcomed, too.

The surgery went well. When I told George about Dr. Pena taking the time to reassure me that God would look after me, George promised he would take me to church every Sunday when I got well. George kept that promise. Ten days later I was in church with my husband beside me. I have missed very few Sundays since.

In the spring of 1986 Geoffrey, now a young man, made plans with his fiancée Stephanie, to marry in April. Wanting to look my best for the occasion, I seriously dieted, colored my hair blonde and was fitted for contact lenses. A professional designer made my dress. I did the best I could to appear presentable as the mother of the groom. Regardless of my efforts, I still came out looking sixty five years old in the wedding pictures, albeit well dressed and smiling. Life was wonderful. Geoffrey has just graduated from SUNY Upstate Medical School and had chosen a beautiful, well educated partner for life.

The summer of '86 passed lazily with plenty of fishing for George and lots of berry picking for me. Friends and family visits were enjoyed. Our weekly square dance sessions kept us on our toes. With the coming of September the days became shorter, the nights became cooler, the grass was wet with early morning dew, the Monarch butterflies had laid their eggs on the milkweed leaves and the geese gathered overhead, ready to fly south. We, too, began to ready ourselves for the annual trek.

George enjoyed one last fishing trip with two men who had come to the campsite without their families because their children were busy with school. The three men headed for the Big Delaware River. That river was too big and fast for anyone to fish alone. George was pleased to have companions to go along. While they were away, I prepared a good dinner for all to enjoy when they returned. I baked an apple pie, made a potato salad and thawed steaks ready for the grill.

On their return George split some wood for the campfire. We all devoured the steak dinner amid stories of fish and fishing. They remarked about George's agility to climb up and down the steep banks, as well as wade waist-deep in the river. "He's no old man!" they declared. As the fire faded and the stars grew brighter, we all retired to our campers. Getting ready for bed George announced, "I have had a perfect day from beginning to end!"

Chapter 12
Widowed 1986

Awaking the next morning, the world was shrouded in fog, thick, thick fog. We always ran into heavy fog on our trips back and forth to the South because we traveled home in the early spring and away in the early fall, the seasons for fog formation. In years past we had had to leave the highway a few times because it was not safe to continue in near zero visibility. Traveling through the Appalachian Mountains in Pennsylvania, Virginia and South Carolina we often encountered dense fog. It made me very nervous. So as I looked out of the window from bed and saw the menacing fog, I commented, "Oh, look at that awful fog. It's here again just as we are getting ready to travel!"

George put his arms around me and assured me saying, "We'll make it. We always do." As we lay cuddled together, he suddenly moved, jerkily his arm thrust toward the headboard of the bed and he started making a gurgling sound. He had told me about that sound, he had heard it when his Grandfather died. I recognized it from George's description. OH, NO! George had died! Frantically I called for help. The paramedics arrived with the ambulance and took him to the hospital in Walton where he was pronounced dead on arrival. It was the worst day of my life.

Our last picture together 1986

I have very little memory of that day. I know our friends; Howard and Betty came to the hospital and stayed with me until the children arrived. Tom, Pat, Gary and Geoffrey came and took care of the necessary arrangements. I was not myself. I had this strange feeling of being apart from it all, like a stranger watching what was happening.

Patti and Gary took me home with them.. Arrangements had to be made for the Memorial Service and for the cemetery. His body was already at the Medical School in Syracuse from which Geoffrey had graduated. Both George and I signed pledges while Geoffrey was a medical student for our bodies to go to science. I was fortunate to locate Reverend Little, retired, to lead the service. Sam was the minister who invited us to join the Endwell Methodist Church many years before. Both he and George had been active in helping the youth of Endwell.

The Memorial service was well attended. Friends, relatives, neighbors, and coworkers crowded the room paying their respect to him. I was overwhelmed with the love that was shared with me. He was a good man and a wonderful husband and father. The neighbors on Lorne Drive stepped right in and prepared refreshments for the return of family and friends.

I had ridden to the funeral with Tom. When we stepped out of the car I immediately saw the Hibbard brothers, Gordon and Sprut. They had come to pay their respects. I couldn't believe they were there. My mind flashed back some forty years to the time we were on the farm. It was the Hibbards that came to our rescue whenever we needed help. Here they were again in my darkest hour.

The next day our four sons and grandson went to the campground and emptied the trailer of our personal things. They shared in the disbursement of their Dad's belongings. The guns, the bows and arrows, the fishing equipment and his gear were divided amongst them. They brought the car and my belongings to me. That ended my life with George.

I can't say how or if I ever adjusted to my new life. My children were caring, thoughtful and kind, but hesitated to advise me where, how or what I should do. Gary, my lawyer son-in-law, took care of the paper work. He escorted me through the Social Security Office to determine my benefits. I learned my income would be less than half of the amount we had together, I was not sure if I had enough money to live on my own. I had never in my life been alone. I was afraid I would not make it. Meanwhile, I just stayed on with Patti, Gary and the three young boys.

It was weird. I felt so alone driving down Main Street. There was no one beside me to comment on my driving; too fast, too slow, or too close to the car ahead. Then when I needed gasoline, I drove up beside the pump, lifted the hose, stuck the nozzle into the car's gas tank opening and nothing happened. No gas trickled into the car. I broke down. I just stood there and cried. I was so helpless, alone! The attendant noticed and came out and showed me that the handle needed to be raised to release the gas. I was on my way to becoming independent.

Don't ask me how I made it through those first few weeks. I know I folded a lot of laundry for Patti. I did other tasks as well. Patti was able to accept substitute teaching assignments as long as I was there to watch over young Michael. The days did come and go in their usual rhythm. The world did not stop for my grief.

I received a phone call. It was Gordon Hibbard. He told me that he had lost his wife seven years before. So he knew what I was going through. He asked if he could visit and talk with me. He came the next afternoon. I told him I was sure I would be fine in a year because most widows do adjust eventually. However, I wondered how to make it from today to tomorrow. He said to me, "You can dress in black, pull all the shades, and sit alone in the dark, but that will never bring George back to you. The best thing is to keep going. How about going out to dinner with me?"

Shocked, I replied, "No! I couldn't think of it so soon!" Patti urged me to accept, telling me it would do me good to go out with an old friend. I was talked into it. It really did make me feel better to dress up and put on make-up again. We went to dinner that Saturday and many Saturdays after that.

Another friend, Alice, with whom I had taught school, also paid attention to me. She took me to the Retired Teachers' luncheon and to her quilting club meeting. She suggested taking up quilting as a new hobby. I followed her suggestion and enrolled in a quilting class where we made a wall hanging using nine different patterned squares. I found I liked quilting and so have continued sewing them.

It is surprising how little things can hurt when you are vulnerable. The high school held their homecoming weekend starting with a parade that came up Hooper Road right past our corner. They broke into song as they went by. What did they play? "Don't Get Around Much Anymore". I felt the tears burning in my throat and spilling down my cheeks.

I missed George so much. The last eight years we were inseparable enjoying life to its fullest. Our retirement had been fulfilling for both of us.

The holidays came and went. I was still staying at Patti and Gary's house. Their three young boys brought much joy in celebrating Christmas. Now I must think about going off on my own. I had to get to our property in Florida. Son Paul offered to drive down there with me. He took vacation time to help me. Paul was really good company. He kept me entertained during the three-day drive. After we arrived, he spent the rest of the week helping me raise awnings, settle the porch furniture after being stored in the living room back into the Florida room, mowed the lawn, made sure I was set to spend the rest of the winter there. He flew back to his home and family in Massachusetts.

Now the loneliness really set in. I managed pretty well during the day, spending time at the pool visiting with my snowbird friends. The nights were long and lonely. On square dance night I would attend the dances by myself and dance every dance with a volunteer husband of friends. Going home alone to an empty house was difficult.

Preparing and eating meals alone became a big problem. I would just pop a bag of popcorn in the microwave and eat right out of the bag. Later I solved that problem by inviting company for dinner at least twice a week. Now I could cook a proper meal, enjoy company eating and had leftovers to warm for another meal. My guests would often invite me to dine with them, too.

I received a phone call to pick up a package that was waiting for me at the bus terminal. The package turned out to be Gordon. That was a pleasant surprise. He stayed two weeks. While he was visiting, his sister Betty and husband Tom drove down from Ocala and spent the weekend. It was great to have a house full again. My children could no longer visit because their children were in school.

At Easter time son Tom flew down to help me close up the place and drive back north. I had made it through the winter! Upon returning to Patti's in Endwell, Gordon and I resumed going out to dinner. I suggested we do something more than just eat, something like dancing, square dancing. In the fall he agreed to attend lessons that were held at the high school right there in Whitney Point. I would drive the twenty some miles on Tuesday evenings to be his partner for the class. I did not care that it was beginning level; I liked to dance no matter the level.

As the days grew shorter and the weather grew worse it worried me to drive on the slippery, icy roads. One night a snow storm hit while we were dancing. That did it. I stayed the night at his house in Triangle. Since his bedroom was on the main floor, the upstairs bedrooms were used only when one of his daughters stayed overnight. I had my choice of which room I wished to sleep in. There was a full bath on the second floor. That worked out so well, I would plan on staying over on dance night. That expanded to dinner, dance and stay the night.

By the time spring arrived, I was spending more and more time with Gordon. Together we planted an enormous vegetable garden and also some flower gardens. He seemed to enjoy the help and my company. His house sat in the beautiful countryside of rolling hills. The scenery was a picture-postcard stereotype with the tall white steeple of the Triangle Baptist Church rising among the hills. The view was always inspiring regardless of the season.

Gordon's house and gardens at Triangle, NY 1990

That spring Maine-Endwell School District and the Kiwanis Club honored George by naming the annual Invitational Relay Races for him. He had coached track teams for more than thirty years at Endwell, many of them championships. I was invited to present the ribbons and trophies to the winners. I accepted the honor and for several years repeated the ritual.

With Gordon as a companion, I was once again able to travel. We took a sojourn to Mount Washington, New Hampshire to ride the cog train. We visited my brother Ralph's family in Vermont and called on relatives of Gordon's at Paris, Maine. We called on a few New Englanders that were also snowbird square dancers.

I also spent time with each of my children. Tom was living in a sparsely furnished apartment since his divorce. I suggested we purchase a house together since both of us needed a home. It didn't take long to find an attractive raised ranch house in Camillus, New York. We agreed for me to make the down payment and Tom took the responsibility of the mortgage payments. Christmas was spent in our new house with Tom's children, Jessica and Andrew. I became

154

much closer to those grandchildren because they spent the weekends with their Dad and me.

Camillus, NY 1989

That winter Gordon drove to Florida with me. It would be the last time I would winter at the Goldcoaster. I planned on selling the winter home because I was only using it three months out of the year and the upkeep, caretaker and utility bills were costly. We spent those last months revisiting the places I had so enjoyed for the past eight years. We went crabbing in the Everglades, picnicking at Bayfront Park, rode the Conch Train at Key West, and searched for the Fountain of Youth in St. Augustine. Farmer Gordon was interested in the huge growing fields. We visited a tomato packing house and watched as the huge trucks loaded with green tomatoes were emptied into tanks of warm water to wash. Then rising on a conveyer belt from their bath to automatic sorters as the attendants quickly removed any tomato having color. They were boxed as green tomatoes of uniform size. The boxes continued on the belt to the gas chamber where they were stacked, then gassed to semi-ripening and finally loaded into trailer trucks from which they were delivered up north, still firm and now red enough to be sold at the supermarket. Another fascinating sight was the mountain of tomatoes that had been unloaded at the tomato dump because they were too ripe and unfit to ship.

155

When March came I began packing my things for leaving. I sold the house with the furniture, at a handsome profit, I might add. All of my personal and favorite things needed to go to the house in Camillus. There was too much to make it in one trip, so I packed a box or two each day and ran them to the United Parcel Service for shipping. This packing and shipping went on for three weeks. Tom called to assure me that my belongings were arriving. He also told me that the police had come to the house and examined the boxes. Apparently, UPS reported to them that something suspicious was arriving daily from southern Florida. It was only me, soon to come home.

That spring and summer Tom and I really went to town on our newly purchased house. We removed built-in book cases from one wall in the living room, washed and painted the walls and even refinished the hard wood floors. A visit to the Ethan Allen Furniture Store provided our interior furnishings and draperies. When all was in place, it became a comfortable, livable, attractive home. It was also a pleasure to be living near two of my sisters, Carol and Betty.

Just two blocks from the house was a quilt shop located in a plaza. I was in my glory. I signed up for classes where I learned a lot and made some very nice quilts and a few dolls and carry all bags. I really threw myself into those classes. Life was good again and getting better.

Gordon liked going south for the hard part of the winter. He located a condo to rent that was near his sister and her husband. Taking my quilting supplies and even my portable sewing machine with us, we trekked back to Florida. The condo was on a golf course. Betty and Tom and Gordon all played, so I bought a set of clubs, took lessons and attempted to play. I was so bad. I loved being out-of-doors in beautiful surroundings with good company, but I just didn't seem to be able to connect with the ball when I took a swing. It was so frustrating!

When I came back home for the summer, Betty and Carol invited me to play in their league. Same problem, couldn't hit the ball. I completed the summer league, but never joined again. I still would play with Gordon, but I chose to play best ball. There were a few times when my ball was the best ball!

That summer Gordon and I drove to Michigan to visit Paul and his family in their new home. They had moved from the Boston area into a small town outside of Detroit. They were a happy family with their two lovely young daughters. We toured the Ford Museum while visiting them.

Now all of my children were on their very own. I would spend time with each one of them by flying here and there as their schedules would permit. There were still places to go and things to do. My sister Edith and her husband Arthur had retired to Wyoming to be near their older son. Well, that just made one more place to visit. Who wants to travel alone? Not I, so I packed up two of my grandchildren, Matthew and Jessica and off we flew to discover the West.

We ran into difficulty when the plane we were to board in Detroit failed to arrive. The airline offered us first class accommodations the next day. I called Paul and he came and took us home for the night at his house. The cousins, all about ten years old, had a chance to play together.

First class travel was remarkable. Snacks, soft drinks, games and a deck of cards were offered along with the free movie. The children were spoiled by the service. We had to change planes again at Chicago. During the wait for boarding Matthew checked the change return slot on every pay telephone while Jessica, a gymnast, did cartwheels through O'Hare Airport.

They were lively for the next ten days as Edith and Arthur

escorted us on day trips into the Bighorn Mountains where they leaped from pinnacle to pinnacle on the rocks as I panicked. We visited a sheep fold and Medicine Wheel where Jessica left a piece of her jewelry at the Indian Burial Grounds. Next it was on to Yellowstone where we stayed overnight in a cabin. They dared to see how close they could come to the hot springs and the wild animals. They enjoyed the excursion. I was nervous most of the time. However, we all returned to our homes safe and sound.

My life had settled into place. I had a warm, comfortable home with Tom. I had a good friend and companion in Gordon. I had a big garden to work in. I had my needlework of quilting and knitting. A pattern developed. Although I lived with Tom, I spent a lot of time with Gordon and often visited others. Gordon and I went to Florida for three months each winter. In the summer I was included on vacations by my children. Patti and Gary took me with them when they went to Ocean City. Tom and I took his children and cousins on camping excursions in the Adirondack Mountains. Life was full and rich and good again.

I was even pursued by an old flame from college. The Cortland College alumni office sent me a card stating someone was trying to contact my husband. Since it was near the fifty year reunion I thought he was being asked to serve on a committee. The inquirer's name and address were included. I wrote to him stating that George was no longer living. Then the letters started coming. He professed how much he had always thought of me and could we somehow meet. Sure, I was flattered. The meeting took place while I was with Tom and the kids in the mountains. He was purchasing a retirement home in the mountains and wanted me to see it. It was a spacious log house with a scenic view. We then went to Saratoga for the horse races. He drank quite heavily and he informed me that he had been married three times; only one of his wives had died. He made Gordon look like a prince, by comparison. No other meetings occurred.

April 25th, 1990 we welcomed a new baby into the family. Karolyn was born to Geoffrey and Stephanie. Her father was elated. He couldn't find enough words to express her beauty and his joy! She was a healthy, pretty baby with a mop of dark straight hair. When they came home from the hospital, I visited and stayed a few weeks to help out. How I loved holding that precious new baby.

On June 12th, 1992 Kristie Nicole was born to Jim and his new wife. Gloria. I traveled to Pensacola to hold her. I traveled to Pensacola seven years later to attend her funeral. She had been struck by a car while crossing a busy road.

Another change came into my life when Tom called me while I was visiting at Gordon's to tell me that Jessica had moved in. As a pre-teen she had begun to assert herself making it difficult to remain with her mother. It was suggested I stay at Gordon's until she and Tom established the limits of their personal space. Gordon and I just had more time together.

I had attended his church whenever I was with Gordon. I made friends there. I became an active helper for crafts for the annual bazaar as well as helping with the many church dinners. I attended the United Methodist Women's Society meetings assisting whenever asked. The lifestyle reversed itself, instead of visiting Gordon; I then visited Tom and Jessica. She really bloomed under the guidance of her father. She became active in her high school marching band and the theater group. Her studies improved.

Good friends of Gordon's that I came to know and like from church spent their winters at Colony Cove in New Port Richey, Florida. Rosco and Marge located a rental for us. We had a great time that winter. With them and seven other couples we took a cruise, visited Disney World and Busch Gardens. I began line dance lessons and the daily exercise

159

classes. We also played pinochle whenever there wasn't an activity scheduled. It was busy and fun. We rented at Colony Cove every winter after that.

Also wintering at New Port Richey were Edith and Arthur. We lunched together many times. Brother Paul and wife, Margaret, lived outside Jacksonville where he directed a religious affiliated retirement community. Gordon and I, along with Edith and Arthur, spent a few Sundays with them. Once again life was great.....but not forever.

Chapter 13
On My Own 1997

Tom's employer was shutting down the Camillus facility and he was moved to Fort Wayne, Indiana. The house had to be sold. That was the easy part. It didn't even make it to market. I had to cut two week's off the winter stay to come back and sign the sale papers. I couldn't afford to make the mortgage payments and pay the utility bills and taxes if I tried to keep the house. I didn't want to start over in Indiana where I knew no one. What would I do? Gordon rescued me. He said, "Just stay with me. You are here most of the time anyway." So my things were put into storage. Tom bought a brand new house in Indiana for himself and Jessica.

The last of the grandchildren was born February 27, 1993. Julia may be the last, but she may also be the best. She and I enjoy being together. Now my family has been completed. Our five children have given me fifteen grandchildren: Jonathan, David, Eric, Matthew, Jennifer, Jessica, Stephen, Rachel, Bryan, Andrew, Michael, Michael, Karolyn, Kristie, and Julia. They are enough to fill any woman's heart.

Thanksgiving, 1998

Back on the farm, Gordon celebrated his eightieth birthday. He was diagnosed with prostate cancer and was treated. He was put on blood thinner for an arrhythmic heart condition. He had both of his knees replaced. He had had to slow down. He wanted to sell and move into the tenant house next door to his son.

Meanwhile, Geoffrey wanted me to come to Rochester in my role as grandmother. He always loved his grandmother and wanted his girls to know their grandmother. I was visiting their family when I saw a well-kept apartment complex and said, "I wouldn't mind living in there. I wonder if I could afford the rent." Right away Stephanie arranged for me to see an apartment. I was pleased with what I saw, went to the manager and rented one that was being renovated. I moved in August of 2000 and have been contented ever since. I was now living independently for the first time ever and making it.

Stephanie showed me the way to the Pinegrove Senior Center where I could go to take exercise classes and continue line dancing. My first new friend I met in line dancing. She lived in a different building of the apartment complex. It was a chilly day that she and her friend walked past my building. Recognizing Irma from dance class, I opened the window and invited them to join me in a cup of tea. She thought I was daft asking strangers into my home. She didn't realize how lonesome I was for company. My family was busy with their own lives. I couldn't expect them to entertain me. To make sure we stayed close I insisted on the weekly ritual of family night where they came to dinner and afterwards played games.

I became useful by driving the girls to and from dancing classes. While driving down Clinton Street I noticed the cross and flame symbols of the United Methodist Church on a white building. The very next Sunday I attended service there. It was near the end of summer when few people were in attendance. To myself I remarked, "If I choose this church I will really be busy because there are so few members." The next Sunday I attempted to find the Asbury United Methodist Church. That was a big church with a big congregation. I had consulted the road map, but still got lost. I took a quick check of the time on my wrist watch and decided I still had time to get to the small local church. People smiled at me making me feel welcome. After the service a lady came up to me and said, "My name is Dorothy and I'm in charge of you. We're going to the church hall for fellowship and refreshments". I settled there. My life became enriched with new friends who offered invitations to join their book club, theater-attending group, and a bridge club.

My two granddaughters, Karolyn and Julia, attended Catholic school. The private school needed volunteers. I did my part by helping in the school library. That soon expanded into individual testing and tutoring the second and third grade students.

Life was busy, productive and pleasurable when one morning in September I turned on the television to get the weather and news. I was shocked at the picture on the screen. An airplane was protruding from one of the twin towers of the New York City building, the World Trade Center. As I watched, another airplane flew at and into the same building! It was September 11, 2001. The news reported yet another airplane headed for Washington. Those passengers gave their lives overcoming the hijackers, who had taken over the plane to use it as a missile on the White House. Our country no longer seemed safe and secure.

These defiant acts were planned and carried out by a rebel group of Muslims called al-Qaeda who were willing to die as martyrs for Islam. This group had training camps in Afghanistan. In retaliation for this carnage, the United States declared war to rid the area of these radicals. They then

163

entrenched into camps in Iraq causing an expansion of the war against mass destruction. The governments of those countries were quickly deposed, but unrest continued. Daily, these martyrs gave their lives as human bombs. It became a religious war and even more a civil war between sects; Shi'ites and Sunnis. The land that was known as the 'cradle of civilization" became the "cradle of unrest", the battleground between religious and secular control, a culture war.

Geoffrey and his family had big plans for their summer vacation and invited me to join in. We flew to Salt Lake City where a rented motor home was waiting for us to travel to the Teton Mountains and on to Yellowstone Park. Anyone who has traveled in that part of the country knows how empty is seems for miles and miles in Utah, Idaho and Wyoming. At one point Geoffrey stopped the motor home and had us all get out. He invited us to listen, and then asked, "What do you hear?" The reply almost in unison was, "Absolutely nothing!" He loved the empty spaces and tranquility.

During the endless miles of driving the high plains of Wyoming, Julia said, "Gigi, tell me a story about when you were a little girl". When I finished she wanted a story about her daddy when he was a baby. This storytelling went on every time we traveled long distances between the sights.

In the Tetons the family went horseback riding, rafted through the white water, fished, and counted 22 bald eagles. Then it was back to the story telling on the way to Yellowstone Park. Our vacation concluded with a long side-trip to Powell, Wyoming to visit my sister Edith and her ninety five year old husband, Arthur. More story telling over those miles.

A few weeks after we had returned from the vacation, I went to Endwell to visit Patti and her family for the weekend.

164

When I returned there sat a desk and a computer in my bedroom waiting for me to write down all of those stories I told on our trip. Geoffrey set me upon this task. I have the knowledge of typing on a standard typewriter, but I was clueless about using a computer. I had to take classes.

Just one year later I had my own personal attack. Once again I faced surgery to remove cancer from my colon. A routine colonoscopy discovered the growth. That was the third invasion of cancer that I have had to battle. The first was uterine cancer in 1975, the second colon cancer in 1984, and now another colon cancer twenty years later. This time I had my doctor son with me all the way. He gave me the assurance that all would go well. The surgery was successful but I did not recover well due to the lack of nursing care in the hospital. The intravenous line had to be reinserted, I blacked out from my blood pressure medication and an infection started on the incision. Geoffrey signed me out of the hospital, took me home to my own comfortable bed and stayed with me. He dosed me with antibiotics and removed the infected staples from the surgical wound. He used his vacation time to get me well. He more than repaid me for helping him reach his goal in life. Patti came and cared for me for a week and then Tom took a turn. By the time Tom came, I was well enough to do the cooking for him.

I was completely well when spring came and I could again get out in my flower gardens that border my apartment building. I now have forty one different plants blooming from early spring to late fall, beginning with yellow daffodils nodding their heads and ending with clusters of multi-colored mums. I have won the garden prize offered by the owners of the manor apartments two years in a row.

I am now in my eighty-third year of my life. My younger sister Betty is all that remains from our full house of childhood. Most of my friends from school have passed on.

I have been a widow for twenty years. I have five children and fourteen grandchildren.

I have a few principles I truly believe in for living. First is health. Good health enables one to live a full life without restrictions or pain. I am blessed with no pain and the ability to exercise daily. Then there is faith. Faith guides us in our daily decisions and offers solace in time of need. Next there is service. Service fulfills our need to be useful and to enhance others. Then there is love. Love does make the world go 'round. Love makes life worth living.

This is my story. What is yours?

09/06/2005 (83rd birthday)

When Jeanette was born her family did not possess a radio or car, and music was played on a Victrola. Only stunt pilots flew planes.

A man landed on the moon twenty seven years ago. Today this biography was written on a PC, copied to a "jump drive", and the old pictures were scanned digitally onto a CD. Her grandchildren listen to iPods, do their homework on wireless laptops and talk with their friends not by phone but by AOL instant messenger. Cell phones are the norm, and the cable company provides cable, internet, and telephone service. A lot has occurred in the last 83 years. What remains is the testimony of Jeanette's love of her family, willingness to put herself out for others and her desire to remain active.

Your children should be so lucky to have a life half as full as yours. We love you Mom,

Jim, Tom, Paul, Patti, and Geoff

Bibliography

<u>Our Glorious Century</u>, Reader's Digest Association, Pleasantville, NY, 1994

To: Marcia

Enjoy living!

Jeanette Morris

CPSIA information can be obtained at www.ICGtesting.com
Printed in the USA
BVOW08s1846280616

453803BV00001B/28/P

9 781847 282965